Mary Engelbreit's

'Tis the Season

Holiday Cookbook

ILLUSTRATED BY MARY ENGELBREIT

Photographs by Alison Miksch

Andrews McMeel
Publishing

Kansas City

Mary Engelbreit's *'Tis the Season Holiday Cookbook* © 2000 by Mary Engelbreit Ink

All photography © 2000 by Alison Miksch

For information, write Andrews McMeel Publishing,

an Andrews McMeel Universal company, 4520 Main Street, Kansas City, Missouri 64111.

www.andrewsmcmeel.com

www.maryengelbreit.com

 is a registered trademark of Mary Engelbreit Enterprises, Inc.

Library of Congress Cataloging-in-Publication Data

Engelbreit, Mary.

Mary Engelbreit's 'tis the season holiday cookbook/illustrated by Mary Engelbreit ;

photographs by Alison Miksch.

p. cm.

Includes index.

ISBN 0-7407-0586-5 (hardcover)

1. Christmas cookery. I. Title.

TX739.2.C45 E53 2000

641.5'68--dc21   00-021313

First U.S. Edition

00 01 02 10 9 8 7 6 5 4 3 2 1

Recipe developers: Lori Longbotham & Judith Sutton

Editor: Sarah Stewart

Designer: Lisa E. Vega

Printed in the United Kingdom

Produced by Smallwood & Stewart, Inc., New York City

table of contents

introduction

HANKSGIVING TURKEY! SWEET POTATOES AND STUFFING! Cheesecakes and chocolates and gingerbread cookies! There are many reasons for celebrating the holidays, and one of my favorites is tied directly to the pleasures of the table. Every year I look forward to renewing my love affair with the dishes I've enjoyed since I was a girl, and discovering new treats for my family and friends.

In this book, I've gathered my favorite recipes for the holiday foods I love. Some are as old-fashioned as gingerbread cookies, others are brand new offerings tracked down by shopping on the Web. But each and every one is divinely satisfying. Whether you're the chef in your house (like my husband, Phil, is in ours) or just an enthusiastic connoisseur (as I am), I hope you will enjoy flipping through these pages, putting together an amazing feast, and sharing it with your loved ones.

Happy Holidays!

Mary

Chapter One

appetizers

walnut & port
cheddar spread

ONLY SCROOGE COULD RESIST THE CHARMS of this oh-so-very-English spread, handy to have at the ready for holiday drop-in guests. Port perfectly complements Cheddar, and when you include a rich black bread like pumpernickel: greater perfection. Make the spread at least two days in advance, so that the rich flavors have time to blend.

1 pound Cheddar cheese, cut into 1-inch pieces

¼ cup (½ stick) unsalted butter, at room temperature

¼ cup sour cream

2 tablespoons Port or Madeira wine (optional)

¼ teaspoon ground mace

⅛ teaspoon ground red pepper

1 cup chopped toasted walnuts

Assorted crackers and thinly sliced black bread

1. In the bowl of a food processor, combine the cheese, butter, sour cream, Port, if desired, mace, and ground red pepper, and process until smooth, scraping down the sides of the processor bowl if necessary. Using a spatula, transfer the mixture to a crock or a bowl and stir in the walnuts.

2. Store the spread, covered and chilled, for at least 2 days before serving. Serve it in the crock at room temperature, with an assortment of crackers and bread.

Makes about 3 cups

Don't be caught off guard! Have a variety of easy appetizers and drinks on hand for holiday entertaining. Might we suggest:

- a few bowls of marinated Spanish and Greek olives, spiced with crushed green peppercorns and tarragon or rosemary
- salted toasted nuts and pumpkin seeds
- radishes dipped in softened sweet butter and served with toast
- marinated artichoke hearts
- apples, pears, grapes, and pieces of blue and soft-ripening cheeses, like Stilton or Camembert, respectively
- crostini (tiny rounds of toast topped with anchovy paste, cheese, or pâté)
- sparkling water
- winter wines like Beaujolais Nouveau, California Zinfandel, Gewürztraminer, and of course, Champagne

parmesan & fennel
cheese straws

iF YOU CAN DO THE TWIST, YOU CAN MAKE these. The secret is frozen puff pastry, one of the greatest inventions in the history of civilization. Half the fun is how you serve them: either in a basket lined with a colorful cloth or fanned out like a bouquet in a clear glass or funky old measuring cup. If you make the variation with pepper, best to keep it out of children's hands.

One 17¼-ounce package frozen puff pastry,
thawed according to package directions

¾ cup (about 3 ounces) freshly grated
Parmesan cheese

1 tablespoon fennel seeds

1. Preheat the oven to 400°F.

2. On a lightly floured work surface, unfold 1 puff pastry sheet. Sprinkle ¼ cup of the cheese over the bottom half of the sheet, leaving a ¼-inch border along the edges. Sprinkle 1½ teaspoons of the fennel seeds evenly over the cheese. Fold the pastry sheet half with no cheese and fennel over the other half and sprinkle 2 more tablespoons of cheese over the top. With a floured rolling pin, roll out the pastry to a 14- x 7-inch rectangle. Using a sharp knife, cut the pastry crosswise into ⅓-inch strips.

3. Twist each strip 4 or 5 times and place the strips ¾ inch apart on heavy ungreased baking sheets, gently pressing down on the ends of each strip to keep it twisted. Bake for 11 to 13 minutes, or until golden brown. Let the straws cool on the pan for about 2 minutes. Using a wide spatula, transfer the straws to wire racks to cool completely. Repeat with the remaining pastry, cheese, and fennel seeds.

4. Stored in an airtight container, the cheese straws will keep for several days. Wrap them airtight and they can be frozen for up to 2 weeks. To recrisp frozen straws, reheat them in a 350°F oven for about 5 minutes.

Makes about 7 dozen straws

◆ Cheddar–Black Pepper Cheese Straws

Substitute finely shredded extra-sharp Cheddar cheese for the Parmesan and substitute 1 to 1½ teaspoons coarsely ground pepper for the fennel seeds. Spread ¼ cup plus 2 tablespoons of the cheese over each pastry sheet before folding over, rather than sprinkling any on top afterwards.

rosy applesauce with
crispy latkes

1 ATKES ARE TRADITIONAL FOR CHANUKKAH, but these Eastern European delicacies shouldn't have to wait for a special occasion. They're also just right after a brisk snowman-building competition in the front yard. We suggest serving them with applesauce, but sour cream also hits the spot. Why not both?

APPLESAUCE

4 pounds assorted red apples, such as Stayman (or Winesap), Cortland, McIntosh, Ida Red, or Jonathan, unpeeled and cut into large chunks, including cores and seeds

2 tablespoons sugar, or more to taste

3 tablespoons water

Ground cinnamon, to taste (optional)

LATKES

2 pounds (4 small) baking potatoes

1 cup (2 medium) grated onions

4 large eggs, lightly beaten

¼ cup plus 2 tablespoons all-purpose flour

1 ½ teaspoons salt

1 teaspoon freshly ground pepper

Vegetable oil, for frying

1. Make the applesauce. In a large heavy pot, combine the apples, sugar, and water. Cover and cook over low heat, stirring occasionally, until the apples are very soft, 40 to 50 minutes.

2. Pass the apples through a food mill into a large bowl. Add additional sugar, if needed, and cinnamon, if desired. Serve warm or let cool, cover, and refrigerate until cold. (The applesauce can be made up to 1 day ahead and refrigerated.)

3. Make the latkes. Peel and coarsely grate the potatoes. Put them in a strainer or colander and rinse thoroughly under cold water; drain well. One handful at a time, squeeze the excess moisture from the potatoes and put them into a large bowl. Stir in the onions until well mixed, then stir in the eggs. Stir in the flour, salt, and pepper until well combined.

4. In a large heavy skillet, heat ¼ inch of oil over medium-high heat until hot. Stir the potato mixture well, then add about 2 tablespoons per pancake to the hot oil, flattening the mixture slightly with a spatula; do not crowd the pan. Cook until golden brown on the bottom, about 4 minutes, then carefully turn the pancakes with the spatula and cook until golden brown on the second side, 3 to 4 minutes longer. Transfer to paper towels to drain. Repeat with the remaining potato mixture, stirring it well between batches and adding more oil to the pan if necessary. Serve immediately, with the applesauce.

Serves 8

◆ Scallion Latkes

Substitute 2 bunches scallions, white and light green parts, finely chopped, for the onions.

spicy-sweet nut *brittle*

nOT FOR KIDS, THIS BRITTLE HAS A KICK to it. When you're making the syrup, use a heavy-bottomed saucepan and be sure to stir with a long-handled wooden spoon.

- 2 teaspoons each ground cumin and salt
- 2 cups plus 1 tablespoon sugar
- 1 teaspoon ground coriander
- ½ teaspoon ground red pepper
- ¼ cup apple cider vinegar
- 1 pound toasted blanched whole almonds

1. In a small bowl, combine the cumin, salt, 1 tablespoon sugar, coriander, and ground red pepper; set aside. Lightly grease a large baking sheet and set aside.

2. In a large heavy saucepan, bring the remaining 2 cups sugar and the vinegar to a boil over medium heat. Cook, stirring occasionally, for 15 to 20 minutes, until the mixture turns dark amber and it registers 360°F on a candy thermometer. Remove the saucepan from the heat and add the spice mixture and almonds. Stir until the almonds are evenly coated. Immediately pour the mixture onto the prepared baking sheet and spread with 2 forks to form a single layer of almonds.

3. Cool the brittle completely on the baking sheet on a wire rack. When cool, break the brittle into serving-size pieces.

Makes about 1½ pounds

red pepper *pecans*

mAYBE YOU SHOULDN'T MAKE THESE! Guests tend to fill up on them, and then they have no room left to enjoy your delicious entree! Perhaps the best compromise is to dole them out in limited quantities. If possible, use hot Hungarian paprika, the Rolls-Royce of its class. Don't feel limited to using only pecans either—any nut works well. Organized gift givers (like you?) pack them in fancy old mason or candy jars with a ribbon around the lid and present them as holiday gifts.

- 1 tablespoon unsalted butter
- 2 cups pecans
- ½ teaspoon ground red pepper
- ¼ teaspoon paprika, preferably Hungarian
- ½ teaspoon salt

In a large skillet, melt the butter over medium-low heat. Add the pecans, sprinkle with the ground red pepper, paprika, and salt, tossing to coat evenly. Cook, stirring occasionally, until the nuts are lightly toasted, about 5 minutes. Transfer the pecans to paper towels to drain. Store them in an airtight container at room temperature for up to 1 week.

Makes 2 cups

gremolata-stuffed *cherry tomatoes*

gREMOLATA IS JUST A FANCY NAME FOR A minced parsley, lemon, and garlic blend that traditionally accompanies osso buco. This variation, nestled in tomatoes, is much less of a production. Make these a few hours ahead of time and refrigerate, then bring them back to room temperature before guests arrive.

2 pints cherry tomatoes

Salt

3 tablespoons chopped fresh flat-leaf parsley

2 tablespoons grated lemon zest

2 garlic cloves, minced

Freshly ground pepper

Extra-virgin olive oil

1. With a small sharp knife, cut off just the very top of each tomato. Gently remove the seeds with the handle of a small spoon, and lightly salt the insides of the tomatoes. Drain, cut side down, on paper towels for at least 15 minutes.

2. Mince together the parsley, lemon zest, and garlic. Transfer the mixture to a bowl and season to taste with salt and pepper.

3. Place a pinch of the parsley mixture into each tomato. Drizzle the mixture with just a drop or two of oil; do not use more, or the tomatoes will be messy.

Serves 8

Magical Midnight Supper

In some countries, it's traditional to fast on Christmas Eve, but once the clock strikes midnight, let the feasting begin. The French call the occasion Réveillon, and preparations proceed in earnest all through December 24th. Since everyone is returning after midnight church services, and travelers are arriving late, it's essential to have the food ready and waiting. Simple, warming, informal soup, flaky biscuits, fine-quality dark chocolates, and Champagne should do nicely. A bowl of clementines or blood oranges are always welcome at Christmas Eve. For a little midnight magic, hollow out fresh artichokes, tiny pumpkins, and squash, and insert cream-colored votives inside. Place one at each place setting or group them for a glowing centerpiece.

sour cream & caviar
potato nests

IF EVER AN APPETIZER WAS MADE FOR Champagne, this is it. Potato nests are elegant little finger foods filled with a citrusy sour cream. Choose the caviar your budget allows, from salmon to beluga, or forgo the caviar altogether and substitute a small slice of smoked salmon, each topped with a single parsley leaf. Be prepared for compliments on your innate sense of artistry.

2 large (about 1½ pounds) russet potatoes

½ cup sour cream

2 tablespoons minced fresh parsley

2 teaspoons grated lemon zest

½ teaspoon salt

Pinch of freshly ground pepper

3 ounces caviar

1. In a large saucepan, heat the potatoes and enough cold water to cover to boiling over high heat. Reduce the heat to low, cover, and simmer for 20 minutes, or until the potatoes are just cooked through. Drain the potatoes, cool to room temperature, and refrigerate for at least 1 hour, or until cold.

2. Meanwhile, in a small bowl, stir together the sour cream, parsley, and lemon zest. Refrigerate, covered with plastic wrap, until ready to serve.

3. Preheat the oven to 425°F. Lightly butter thirty-two 1¾-inch mini muffin-pan cups.

4. Peel and coarsely grate the potatoes. In a medium bowl, gently toss the potatoes with the salt and pepper. Place about 1 heaping tablespoon of the potato mixture into each prepared mini muffin-pan cup and press the mixture against the bottom and up the sides of the cup, allowing some mixture to extend slightly above the rim.

5. Bake the potato nests for 25 minutes, or until the edges are dark golden brown. Cool the nests in the pan on wire racks for 10 minutes. Carefully remove the potato nests from the pans and transfer them to a baking sheet lined with paper towels to drain. Let stand at room temperature for up to 4 hours before serving.

6. Preheat the oven to 375°F. Place the potato nests on a large baking sheet (without the paper towels) and bake for 6 to 8 minutes, or until heated through and crisp. Transfer the nests to a platter. Spoon about 1 teaspoon of the sour cream mixture into each potato nest and top each with a scant teaspoon of caviar. Serve immediately.

Serves 8

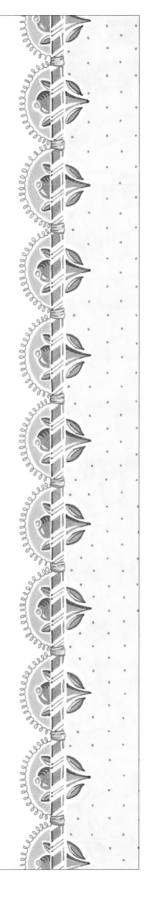

double-sauced
smoked fish platter

WE SEE THIS DISH ON A NEW YEAR'S EVE buffet, with guests distractedly trying different garnishes, completely ignoring the countdown on TV. Why? Because it's so delicious, with each bite just a little bit different, depending on the garnish. Another option is to prepare individual servings as a first course to a Chanukkah or Christmas meal. When in doubt about which fish to choose, go with everyone's favorite: smoked salmon.

MUSTARD-DILL SAUCE

¼ cup Dijon mustard

1 ½ tablespoons finely chopped fresh dill

1 tablespoon fresh lemon juice

⅓ cup vegetable oil

Generous pinch of salt

Freshly ground pepper, to taste

HERBED CRÈME FRAÎCHE

One 8-ounce container crème fraîche or
   sour cream

2 tablespoons vodka

Generous 2 tablespoons minced fresh chives

Salt and freshly ground pepper, preferably white,
   to taste

1 ½ pounds sliced smoked salmon, sturgeon, sable,
   and/or other fish

OPTIONAL GARNISHES

Fresh dill sprigs or chopped fresh chives

Minced red or white onions

Chopped hard-boiled eggs (whites and yolks
   chopped separately)

Capers

Lemon wedges

Thinly sliced brioche and pumpernickel or
   other dark bread

1. Make the mustard-dill sauce. In a small bowl, combine all the ingredients. Cover with plastic wrap and refrigerate until ready to serve. (The sauce can be prepared 1 day in advance.)

2. Make the herbed crème fraîche. In a small bowl, combine the crème fraîche, vodka, and chives. Season with salt and pepper. Cover with plastic wrap and refrigerate until ready to serve. (The crème fraîche can be prepared up to 8 hours ahead.)

3. To serve, arrange the smoked fish on a large platter. Garnish with the dill sprigs, if using, and serve with the mustard-dill sauce, crème fraîche, and any of the other optional garnishes on the side.

Serves 8

ginger-garlic
skewered shrimp

WHEN YOU TIRE OF TRADITIONAL HOLIDAY foods, this lively Asian-inspired dish will deliver a refresher course to your taste buds. It really stimulates the appetite, which is exactly what an appetizer is supposed to do!

4 slender scallions

4 plum tomatoes, seeded and chopped

4 teaspoons fresh lemon juice

4 teaspoons finely chopped peeled ginger

2 garlic cloves, chopped

1 fresh or jarred pickled jalapeño pepper, trimmed, seeded, and finely chopped

2 teaspoons brown sugar

½ teaspoon salt

24 jumbo shrimp (about 2 pounds), peeled and deveined

1. Soak 2 dozen 7-inch bamboo skewers in cold water for at least 30 minutes.

2. Mince the scallions, keeping the white and green parts separate. In the bowl of a food processor, combine the scallion whites, the tomatoes, lemon juice, ginger, garlic, jalapeño, sugar, and salt, processing until well combined. Transfer the mixture to a large bowl, add the shrimp, and let marinate at room temperature, turning frequently, for 20 minutes. Thread the shrimp on the skewers, 1 shrimp per skewer.

3. Heat the broiler. As close to the heat as possible, cook the shrimp on a broiler pan about 1 or 2 minutes per side, just until cooked through and opaque; do not overcook.

4. Serve hot or at room temperature on the skewers, sprinkled with the reserved minced scallion greens.

Serves 8

pastrami-cured
salmon

d ON'T YOU JUST LOVE RECIPES WHERE ALL the work goes into the marinating? Seasoned with traditional pastrami spices, this is no ordinary salmon. We can't think of anything more festive for a Chanukkah celebration—but be prepared to share the recipe with dazzled guests.

APPETIZERS

One 2-pound center-cut salmon fillet with skin

¼ cup kosher salt

¼ cup sugar

1 bunch cilantro, leaves and tender stems only,
   coarsely chopped

1 tablespoon vodka

1 tablespoon coarsely ground black pepper

1 tablespoon cracked or coarsely ground
   white pepper

1 ½ teaspoons ground coriander

½ teaspoon paprika

¼ teaspoon ground allspice

¼ teaspoon ground red pepper

2 teaspoons vegetable oil

HERBED SOUR CREAM (OPTIONAL)

One 8-ounce container sour cream

¼ cup packed finely chopped fresh cilantro, plus a
   few small sprigs, for garnish

Salt, to taste

1. Using tweezers or needle-nose pliers, remove any pinbones from the salmon. Place the salmon, skin side up, on a large sheet of plastic wrap. Combine the salt and sugar in a cup and rub some of the mixture evenly over the skin side of the salmon. Turn the salmon over and cover with the remaining mixture. Scatter the cilantro over the top and sprinkle the vodka over it. Wrap the salmon in the plastic, place in a heavy-duty resealable plastic bag, squeeze out the excess air, and seal the bag. Put the salmon in a baking dish, place a smaller baking dish on top of it, and weight with a 4- to 5-pound weight. Refrigerate the salmon, turning it several times, for 48 hours, or until it is translucent throughout.

2. In a small bowl, combine the black and white pepper, coriander, paprika, allspice, and ground red pepper. Remove the salmon from the marinade and wipe it dry with paper towels. Rub the oil over the flesh side of the salmon, then rub the spice mixture evenly over the flesh. Cover and refrigerate for 2 hours, or until ready to serve.

3. Make the herbed sour cream, if desired. In a small bowl, combine the sour cream, chopped cilantro, and salt. Cover and refrigerate until ready to serve.

4. Using a very sharp knife and holding it at an angle to the cutting board, cut the salmon into very thin slices. Arrange the slices on a platter and serve with the herbed sour cream, if you've made it, garnished with cilantro sprigs.

Serves 8

Chapter Two

soups & salads

THE QUEEN OF THE KITCHEN

smoky butternut

squash soup

WE SPECIFY BUTTERNUT SQUASH BECAUSE it's so sweet, but the truth is you could make this soup with any winter squash you like. Why not brew up a batch in advance—as much as two days ahead—so you'll be ready to kick off the weekend when guests arrive. When reheating, thin the soup with a little chicken stock or water.

4 slices bacon

3 pounds (about 2 small) butternut squash

3 tablespoons unsalted butter

2 large onions, coarsely chopped

2 small carrots, halved lengthwise and
    thinly sliced

2 small celery stalks, thinly sliced

2 garlic cloves, minced

¾ teaspoon salt, or more to taste

3¾ cups chicken stock or low-sodium chicken broth

2 tablespoons thinly slivered fresh sage
    or 2 teaspoons dried

¼ teaspoon freshly ground pepper

1. In a Dutch oven or large heavy pot, cook the bacon over medium-low heat, stirring occasionally, until golden brown and crisp. Using a slotted spoon, transfer the bacon to paper towels to drain, then crumble and set aside. Pour off and discard the fat from the pot and set the pot aside.

2. Meanwhile, cut the butternut squash in half lengthwise and scrape out the seeds. Cut each half lengthwise in half again and, using a sharp paring knife, peel the squash. Cut the squash into ¾-inch chunks.

3. Melt the butter in the pot over medium heat. Add the onions, carrots, celery, garlic, and ¼ teaspoon salt and cook, stirring, until the onions are translucent, 10 to 12 minutes. Add the squash and stock and bring to a simmer. Partially cover and simmer, stirring occasionally, until the squash is very tender, about 15 minutes.

4. In batches, puree the soup in a blender until smooth and return to the pot. Stir in the sage, and season with the remaining ½ teaspoon salt and the pepper. Reheat over medium heat, stirring occasionally, until hot. Ladle into bowls and sprinkle some of the crumbled bacon in the center of each serving.

Serves 8

creamy cheddar
cauliflower soup

Y OU SAY YOUR FAMILY DOESN'T LIKE cauliflower? You say your family refuses to eat cauliflower? This soup will change their attitude. It's so good, it doesn't even need the Cheddar cheese. For a splurge, you could serve it (cheeseless) with a topping of caviar instead. Midnight refrigerator raiders will enjoy it chilled, at the kitchen table with crusty bread.

SOUPS & SALADS

1 ½ tablespoons unsalted butter

1 large onion, finely chopped

3 ¾ cups chicken stock or two 14 ½-ounce
   cans low-sodium chicken broth

1 head cauliflower, cored and separated into
   small florets

1 Yukon Gold or all-purpose potato, peeled
   and coarsely chopped

1 teaspoon salt, or to taste

⅛ teaspoon freshly ground pepper

1 ½ cups heavy cream or half-and-half

½ to 1 cup (2 to 4 ounces) grated
   Cheddar cheese

Chopped chives, for garnish (optional)

1. In a large heavy pot, melt the butter over medium heat. Add the onion and cook, stirring, until it is translucent, 8 to 10 minutes. Add the stock, cauliflower, potato, salt, and

pepper and bring to a boil over high heat. Reduce the heat and boil gently, stirring occasionally, until the cauliflower and potato are very tender, about 18 to 20 minutes. Remove the pot from the heat.

2. In batches, puree the soup in a blender until smooth. (The soup can be made up to this point up to 2 days ahead. Let the soup cool completely, cover with plastic wrap, and refrigerate.)

3. Return the soup to the pot and stir in the cream. Heat over medium-low heat until hot (do not boil), then gradually stir in the cheese until melted and smooth. Transfer the soup to a tureen, and serve immediately, liberally garnished with chopped chives, if desired.

Serves 8

quick & easy

peanut soup

PEANUT SOUP IS AFRICAN IN ORIGIN, MAKing it ideal as a course for a Kwanzaa celebration. Serve it, too, at a relaxed New Year's Day lunch, as you sit around the fire declaring your resolutions before witnesses. Since peanuts are as American as peanut butter, it's almost a sure thing that the kids will love it too. If you have vegetarian guests, replace the chicken stock with vegetable stock or broth.

1½ tablespoons peanut or vegetable oil

1 large onion, finely chopped

2 garlic cloves, minced

¾ teaspoon salt, or more to taste

¾ teaspoon ground red pepper

3¾ cups chicken stock or two 14½-ounce cans
   low-sodium chicken broth

1½ cups smooth peanut butter

1 cup half-and-half

4 scallions, white and light green parts only,
   thinly sliced, for garnish

1. In a large heavy pot, heat the oil over medium-high heat. Add the onion and cook, stirring, until very soft, about 10 to 12 minutes.

2. Add the garlic, salt, and ground red pepper. Cook, stirring constantly, until very fragrant, about 1 minute. Add the stock and bring to a boil. Reduce the heat and simmer for 5 minutes. Whisk in the peanut butter until smooth. Add the half-and-half and heat through. (The soup can be made up to 2 days ahead. Allow it to cool completely, cover with plastic wrap, and refrigerate. Reheat the soup slowly over low heat before serving.)

3. To serve, adjust the seasoning if necessary, then ladle into serving bowls and garnish with the scallions.

Serves 8

southwestern

corn chowder

PICTURE THIS: THE FAMILY, BEARING TIGHT smiles and gifts, have just arrived from their long and traffic-snarled car trip halfway across the state. Grandma's getting testy. The kids are tired and bored. But you, cleverly, have this steaming creamy chowder to soothe away their travel travails. If you think the kids might indulge, skip the jalapeño peppers.

5 slices bacon, cut crosswise into ¼-inch strips

1 large onion, cut into ¼-inch dice

1 large red bell pepper, cored, seeded, and cut into ¼-inch dice

1 poblano pepper, cored, seeded, and minced (optional)

1 to 2 jalapeño peppers, to taste, minced

4 cups chicken stock or two 14½-ounce cans low-sodium chicken broth plus ⅓ cup water

1 pound Yukon Gold or all-purpose potatoes, peeled and cut into ½-inch cubes

3 cups fresh or thawed frozen corn

¾ teaspoon salt, or to taste

⅛ teaspoon freshly ground pepper, or to taste

¾ cup heavy cream

3 tablespoons finely chopped fresh cilantro

1. In a Dutch oven or large heavy pot, cook the bacon over medium heat, stirring occasionally, until golden brown and crisp. Using a slotted spoon, transfer the bacon to paper towels to drain. There should be about 1 tablespoon fat remaining in the pot; pour off any excess.

2. Add the onion, bell pepper, poblano, if desired, and jalapeños to the pot and cook over medium heat, stirring frequently, until the onion is translucent, 8 to 10 minutes. Add the stock and potatoes and bring to a boil over high heat. Reduce the heat and boil gently until the potatoes are almost tender, 8 to 10 minutes. Add the corn and cook until the potatoes are tender but still hold their shape, about 5 minutes.

3. Reduce the heat to low. Transfer about ½ cup of the corn and potatoes, along with about ½ cup of the broth, to a blender and puree until smooth. Return the puree to the pot and stir until well blended. Season with the salt and pepper; stir in the cream and reserved bacon. Heat the soup through (do not let boil). Adjust the seasoning if necessary. Stir in the cilantro and serve.

Serves 8

tomato & rice
shrimp bisque

tHE TREE IS TRIMMED. YOU'VE MANAGED to assemble the radio airplane, and you actually remembered to get the right kind of batteries for the toy robot. Your reward? A cozy midnight supper kicked off with this marvelously smooth bisque. Throw on a confetti of parsley or chives, or just use a single elegant shrimp for garnish.

6 tablespoons (¾ stick) butter

1½ pounds medium shrimp, peeled and deveined
   (reserve the shells)

2 cups water

1 cup dry white wine

1 large onion, coarsely chopped

2 carrots, peeled and coarsely chopped

2 celery stalks, coarsely chopped

¼ cup long-grain white rice

1 bay leaf

1¼ teaspoons salt

¼ teaspoon ground red pepper

One 14½-ounce can diced tomatoes

1 cup heavy cream

1. In a large Dutch oven or large heavy pot, melt 2 tablespoons of the butter over medium heat. Add the shrimp shells and cook, stirring constantly, for 3 minutes, or until they turn pink. Add the water and wine and bring to a boil. Reduce the heat to low and simmer, covered, for 15 minutes. Set a strainer lined with two layers of damp cheesecloth over a medium bowl. Pour the liquid through, pressing on the solids with the back of a wooden spoon to extract as much of the liquid as possible. Discard the solids and set the liquid aside.

2. In the same Dutch oven, melt the remaining 4 tablespoons butter over medium heat. Add the shrimp and cook, stirring, for 2 minutes, or until they turn pink and are just cooked through; do not overcook. With a slotted spoon, transfer the shrimp to a large bowl. Add the onion, carrots, and celery to the pot and cook, stirring, for 10 minutes, or until softened.

3. Add the reserved liquid from the shells, the rice, bay leaf, salt, and ground red pepper and bring the mixture to a boil. Reduce the heat to low and simmer, covered, for 20 minutes, or until the rice is tender. Remove the Dutch oven from the heat. Remove and discard the bay leaf. Stir in the tomatoes and the shrimp.

4. In batches, puree the soup in a blender, reserving 8 shrimp for garnish. (The soup can be prepared ahead to this point, covered and chilled.)

5. Return the soup to the Dutch oven and add the cream. Bring the bisque just to a boil over medium heat, stirring constantly. Ladle the bisque into serving bowls and garnish with the reserved shrimp.

Serves 8

fresh thyme & mushroom soup

eVEN IF IT'S ZERO DEGREES OUTSIDE (with a wind chill making it feel like −35) you can sit back and imagine yourself dining in France when you taste this soup, redolent of earthy mushrooms and aromatic thyme. The soup can be made ahead through step 5, covered, and chilled for up to three days before serving. It will only get better as the flavors intensify.

1 pound small white mushrooms

6 tablespoons (¾ stick) butter

1 teaspoon fresh lemon juice

1 onion, chopped

2 tablespoons all-purpose flour

2 cups water

One 14½-ounce can low-sodium chicken broth

½ teaspoon fresh thyme leaves,
    plus whole sprigs, for garnish

½ teaspoon salt

Freshly ground pepper, to taste

½ cup heavy cream

1. Remove the mushroom stems and set aside. Thinly slice the mushroom caps.

2. In a Dutch oven or large heavy pot, melt 2 tablespoons of the butter over medium-high heat. Add the sliced mushroom caps and the lemon juice and cook, stirring occasionally, for 10 minutes, or until the mushrooms are softened. With a slotted spoon, transfer the mushrooms to a bowl and set aside.

3. Reduce the heat to medium, add the remaining 4 tablespoons butter, the onion, and the mushroom stems. Cook, stirring, for 8 minutes, or until the onion is softened.

4. Add the flour and cook, stirring, for 2 minutes. Gradually stir in the water and broth, then stir in the thyme, salt, and pepper. Bring to a boil over high heat, stirring constantly.

5. In batches, puree the soup in a blender until smooth. Transfer to a large bowl and set aside. Rinse the Dutch oven.

6. Return the mixture to the clean Dutch oven and stir in the cream and the reserved mushrooms. Bring the mixture just to a boil over medium heat. Ladle into bowls and serve hot, garnished with thyme sprigs.

Serves 8

butter lettuce with brie,
red onions & peas

WE SEE YOUR FAMILY ENJOYING THIS SALAD after a long day of holiday shopping. It's a painless way to eat your peas. Dice the Brie while it is still cold, but allow it to come to room temperature before adding it to the salad to let its buttery flavor blossom.

1 ½ tablespoons fresh lemon juice

¼ teaspoon Dijon mustard

¼ cup olive oil

½ teaspoon salt, or more to taste

⅛ teaspoon freshly ground pepper, or more to taste

2 large or 3 medium heads butter lettuce or other soft lettuce, rinsed, dried, and torn into bite-size pieces

Scant 1 cup slivered red onions

1 cup thawed frozen baby peas

8 to 12 ounces Brie, rind removed, if desired, and cut into ½-inch dice

1 small bunch chives, cut into 1-inch lengths (optional)

1. Combine the lemon juice and mustard in a jar, cover tightly, and shake to blend well. Add the oil, salt, and pepper; cover; and shake well to blend.

2. In a large bowl, combine the lettuce, red onions, and peas. Add the dressing, tossing to coat. Arrange the salad on individual plates and scatter the Brie over the top. Sprinkle the chives over, if desired, and serve immediately.

Serves 8

The Happy Holiday Refrigerator

Ever marvel at the people who seem to glide through the weeks leading up to Christmas, getting everything accomplished without seeming the slightest bit stressed—not to mention taking real joy in the season? Now you can count yourself among them:

• In early December, place your order for turkey or roast for Christmas dinner. Ask them to have it ready by the 23rd.

• If just the thought of going out grocery shopping makes you weary, consider markets that will deliver phone orders, catalogs, and food shopping Websites.

• A few extra delicacies tucked into the refrigerator can make your holidays considerably brighter. Go for the best: a tin of caviar, quails' eggs, smoked salmon, and fresh raspberries.

33

grapefruit *salad*

WHEN THE BITTER NORTH WIND DOTH BLOW, fortify yourself with this vitamin-packed salad that's elegant to boot. To add to the allure, you can make it ahead of time.

5 slender scallions

2 tablespoons white wine vinegar

1 teaspoon Dijon mustard

1 garlic clove, mashed to a paste with

½ teaspoon salt

¼ teaspoon freshly ground pepper

½ cup vegetable oil

3 heads Boston lettuce, torn into bite-size

pieces

1 head radicchio, cored and separated into leaves

3 large pink grapefruit, peeled and sectioned

1. Finely chop the scallions, keeping the white and tender green parts separate. In a small bowl, whisk together the scallion whites, vinegar, mustard, garlic mixture, and pepper. Slowly add the oil, whisking, until the vinaigrette is blended.

2. In a large bowl, toss the lettuce and radicchio with the dressing, coating well. Divide the mixture among salad plates. Top each salad with some grapefruit sections and scallion greens. Serve immediately.

Serves 8

fennel salad with *oranges*

FENNEL'S BRISK-AS-A-LICORICE-WHIP TASTE is just so right around the holidays. Very Italian, this salad may have you looking for La Befana instead of Santa.

2 tablespoons olive oil

2 tablespoons fresh lemon juice

2 garlic cloves, mashed to a paste with

½ teaspoon salt

⅛ teaspoon ground red pepper

8 naval oranges

2 small fennel bulbs, trimmed and cut into long

thin strips (feathery tops reserved)

2 small red onions, thinly sliced

1. In a small bowl, whisk together the oil, lemon juice, garlic mixture, and ground red pepper. Set the dressing aside.

2. With a sharp knife, peel the oranges, making sure to remove all the white pith. Cut each orange in half through the stem end and then cut crosswise into slices. In a serving bowl, stir together the oranges, fennel, and red onions until well combined. (The ingredients can be prepared several hours ahead and stored covered and chilled until ready to serve.)

3. Just before serving, finely chop the reserved fennel tops, add them to the orange mixture with the dressing, and toss well to combine. Serve immediately.

Serves 8

traditional holiday
seafood salad

hAVE YOU EVER BEEN TO AN ITALIAN household on Christmas Eve? You MUST try each and every one of the 12 seafood entrees lined up on the sideboard, or your host will be crestfallen. Capture the spirit of the evening without the bulk by making this all-in-one salad—it's much lighter.

½ cup fresh lemon juice (from about 2 lemons)

2 garlic cloves, minced

Salt and freshly ground pepper, to taste

¼ cup fruity olive oil

4 cups water

2 carrots, peeled and chopped

2 small celery stalks with leaves,
    cut into 1-inch lengths

1 lemon, sliced and seeded

12 black peppercorns

1 pound medium shrimp, peeled and deveined

1 pound bay scallops

1 pound cleaned squid, cut into rings

1 pound small mussels, scrubbed and debearded

2 tablespoons minced fresh parsley

Lemon wedges, for garnish

1. In a large bowl, stir together the lemon juice and garlic, and season with salt and pepper. Slowly whisk in the oil until blended. Set aside.

2. In a large Dutch oven, bring the water, carrots, celery, sliced lemon, and peppercorns to a boil over high heat. Reduce the heat to medium and add the shrimp. Cook for 1 to 2 minutes, until pink; do not overcook. With a slotted spoon, transfer the scallops to a large bowl; set the bowl aside. Return the liquid to a boil and add the scallops. Cook for 1 to 2 minutes, until just opaque; do not overcook. With a slotted spoon, remove the scallops and transfer to the bowl with the shrimp. Return the liquid to a boil, add the squid, and cook for 30 seconds. With a slotted spoon, transfer the squid to the bowl.

3. Return the liquid to a boil and add the mussels. Cook, covered, over high heat until most have opened, about 5 minutes. Transfer the opened mussels to a plate and cook any unopened mussels for 1 minute longer. Discard any unopened mussels. Remove the mussels from the shells and add to the bowl with the other cooked seafood.

4. Add the dressing and toss to coat. Cover and refrigerate, stirring occasionally, for about 3 hours, or until cold. (The salad can be prepared ahead and refrigerated for up to 8 hours.)

5. Remove the salad from the refrigerator 30 minutes before serving. Gently stir in the parsley and garnish the salad with the lemon wedges.

Serves 8

watercress & smoked *trout salad*

aREN'T WE GETTING A LITTLE BIT BORED with lettuce right now? Yes, we are. Much more intriguing is a combination of the peppery bite of watercress, the sweetness of sugar snap peas (or try snow peas), and the deep flavor of smoked trout—all served with a glass of Chenin Blanc. You're a genius.

6 ounces sugar snap peas or snow peas, trimmed

1 tablespoon fresh lemon juice

½ teaspoon salt

⅛ teaspoon freshly ground pepper

3 tablespoons olive oil

1 pound smoked trout fillets

2 bunches watercress, tough stems removed

Chopped chives, for garnish (optional)

1. Bring a large saucepan of salted water to a boil. Add the snap peas and cook, stirring once or twice, just until they turn bright green, 30 seconds to 1 minute. Drain immediately and let cool. Slice the peas on the diagonal into ⅓-inch-wide pieces. Set aside.

2. In a small jar, combine the lemon juice, salt, pepper, and olive oil. Cover the jar tightly, and shake well to blend completely. Set aside.

3. Pull the skin off the trout fillets. Using two forks or your fingers, gently separate the fillets into bite-size pieces.

4. Put the watercress and snap peas in a large bowl, add the dressing, and toss well. Add the trout and toss again. Arrange the salad on individual serving plates. Sprinkle with chives, if desired, and serve immediately.

Serves 8

Merry Movie Marathon

Throw a holiday movie marathon party. Invite a few close friends over, fill bowls with munchies or set a buffet, load the videos, and enjoy the show. *It's a Wonderful Life, Miracle on Thirty-Fourth Street, Holiday Inn, White Christmas,* and *How the Grinch Stole Christmas* are all fair game, as is any vintage W.C. Fields' classic. This is also an evening to get some serious tree-trimming done, particularly if you ply your guests with good Champagne and lots of hot hors d'oeuvres.

Chapter Three

main courses

THE QUEEN OF THE KITCHEN

tangy chile &
chicken yassa

aLL THE WAY FROM SENEGAL, WEST AFRICA, this zingy dish is a natural for a Kwanzaa family dinner. We'll admit that the parsley isn't traditional, but it does add a bit of evergreen color. Like all the best chicken dishes, this one benefits from side servings of plenty of steaming hot white rice.

2½ pounds (5 to 6 large) onions, halved
 lengthwise and very thinly sliced

2 to 3 jalapeños or other hot peppers, minced

2 large garlic cloves, minced

¼ cup plus 2 tablespoons fresh lemon juice (from
 about 2 large lemons)

¼ cup plus 2 tablespoons peanut or other
 vegetable oil

Two 3½-pound chickens, cut into serving pieces

Salt and freshly ground pepper, to taste

¾ cup water

3 tablespoons finely chopped fresh flat-leaf parsley

1. In a large bowl, combine the onions, half the jalapeños, the garlic, lemon juice, and oil, tossing to mix well. Put the chicken in a large shallow baking dish and add the onion mixture, turning the chicken to coat. Cover and marinate in the refrigerator for 2 to 4 hours.

2. Preheat the broiler. Remove the chicken from the baking dish, scraping off the onions and reserving the onion marinade, and season on both sides with salt and pepper. Place the chicken, skin side up, on the broiler pan and broil as close to the heat as possible for about 10 minutes, or until golden brown. Turn the chicken over and broil for 5 to 7 minutes longer, or until golden brown on the second side. Remove the chicken from the broiler and set aside.

3. Meanwhile, heat a large Dutch oven over medium-high heat until hot. Add the onion mixture and the remaining jalapeños and cook, stirring occasionally, until the onions are translucent, 10 to 12 minutes. If the onions start to stick, add a tablespoon or so of water.

4. Reduce the heat to medium, add the water and 2 tablespoons of the parsley, and bring just to a simmer. Place the chicken, skin side up, on top of the onions. Partially cover the pot, and simmer gently until the chicken is cooked through, 15 to 20 minutes. Transfer the mixture to a serving dish and sprinkle the remaining 1 tablespoon parsley on top.

Serves 8

mushroom gravy-topped
roasted turkey

WHO NEEDS STUFFING WHEN YOU CAN HAVE an extra-special gravy that's a lot less work? Brimming with paper-thin sliced mushrooms, this creamy gravy perks up the turkey while it emboldens potatoes, such as French-Style Mashed Potatoes (page 94).

> **One 12- to 14-pound fresh or thawed frozen turkey**
> **Salt and freshly ground pepper**
> **About 3 cups chicken broth**
> **One 10-ounce package mushrooms, thinly sliced**
> **1 teaspoon fresh thyme leaves**
> **2 tablespoons all-purpose flour**
> **½ cup heavy cream**

1. Preheat the oven to 350°F.

2. Rinse the turkey inside and out and pat dry. Place the turkey, breast side up, on a rack in a large roasting pan. Tuck the turkey skin at the neck end under the turkey, fold the wings under the back, and, if necessary, tie the legs together with kitchen string. Season the turkey with salt and pepper to taste and cover loosely with foil.

3. Roast the turkey for 2¾ hours, basting every 30 minutes with the pan juices. Remove the foil and continue roasting for about 45 minutes longer, or until an instant-read thermometer inserted into the thickest part of the thigh, away from the bone, registers 180°F.

4. Transfer the turkey to a cutting board and let stand, loosely covered with foil, for about 20 minutes.

5. Meanwhile, pour the pan juices from the roasting pan into a large measuring cup and add enough broth to measure 3 cups. Spoon off 3 tablespoons of the fat from the top and heat it in a large nonstick skillet over high heat. Add the mushrooms and thyme to the skillet and cook, stirring occasionally, until browned, about 10 minutes. Add the flour and cook, stirring constantly, for 1 minute. Add the broth mixture and cream. Bring the mixture to a boil, and cook, stirring occasionally, for 5 to 10 minutes, until slightly thickened. Season to taste with salt and pepper.

6. Carve the turkey and arrange on a serving platter. Transfer the gravy to a sauceboat, and serve on the side.

Serves 8

THERE IS NOTHING MORE PROPERLY THE LANGUAGE OF THE HEART THAN THE WISH.

brine-roasted turkey

fINALLY, YOUR MOMENT OF TRIUMPH IS here. You've waited years to show the family that, yes, you do know how to make a great turkey. This recipe will not fail you: It involves soaking the bird in a salty brine to guarantee succulence. Use only fresh (not frozen) turkeys; prebasted and kosher birds are too salty. Better put in your order at the turkey farm now.

2 gallons (32 cups) water

2 cups kosher salt

2 cups packed brown sugar

2 tablespoons peppercorns, coarsely cracked

One 12- to 14-pound fresh turkey

2 tablespoons unsalted butter, at room temperature

Salt and freshly ground pepper, to taste

1. The night before roasting the turkey, make the brine. In a medium saucepan, combine 4 cups of water, the kosher salt, and the sugar and heat over medium heat, stirring, until the salt and sugar dissolve. Remove the pan from the heat, stir in the peppercorns, and let cool.

2. Rinse the turkey inside and out. Place the turkey in a very large pot and add the remaining 28 cups water and the brown sugar mixture, stirring to blend. If your pot isn't quite large enough, use less water and slightly less of the brown sugar mixture; if the brine doesn't quite cover the turkey, place it breast side up to start, then turn over after a few hours. Refrigerate for 12 to 15 hours.

3. Remove the turkey from the brine, discard the brine, and rinse the turkey thoroughly under cold running water. Pat dry and refrigerate.

4. Preheat the oven to 325°F.

5. Rub the butter all over the turkey and season with salt and pepper. Tuck the turkey wings under the back and, if necessary, tie the legs together with kitchen string. Place the turkey, breast side up, on a rack in a roasting pan and roast, basting every 30 minutes with the pan juices, for 1 hour. Cover the turkey breast loosely with a foil tent and roast for 2½ to 3 hours longer, or until an instant-read thermometer inserted into the thickest part of the thigh, away from the bone, registers 180°F; about 45 minutes before the turkey is done, remove the foil tent. Let the turkey stand, loosely covered with foil, for about 20 minutes before carving.

Serves 8

herb-roasted turkey

JUST THE SCENT OF THE BUTTERY GARLIC-herb mixture that makes this turkey special will have everyone drifting into the kitchen wearing dazed smiles of anticipation. But the aroma is just the prelude: This bird is heaven.

> 5 tablespoons unsalted butter, at room temperature
>
> 3 tablespoons minced fresh parsley
>
> 1 ½ tablespoons minced fresh rosemary
>
> or 2 teaspoons crumbled dried,
>
> plus 3 to 4 large sprigs
>
> 3 garlic cloves, minced
>
> One 12- to 14-pound fresh or thawed frozen turkey
>
> Salt and freshly ground pepper, to taste

1. Preheat the oven to 325°F. In a small bowl, combine 3 tablespoons of the butter, the parsley, the minced rosemary, and garlic and blend well. Rinse the turkey inside and out and pat dry with paper towels. Using your fingertips, carefully separate the skin of the breast and thighs from the flesh, without tearing the skin. Rub the herb-butter mixture evenly over the breast and thigh meat, under the skin, and place the rosemary sprigs inside the turkey cavity. Rub the remaining 2 tablespoons butter over the skin of the turkey and sprinkle with salt and pepper. Tuck the turkey wings under the back and, if necessary, tie the legs together with kitchen string.

2. Place the turkey, breast side up, on a rack in a roasting pan and roast, basting every 30 minutes with the pan juices, for 1 hour. Cover the turkey breast loosely with a foil tent and roast for 2½ to 3 hours longer, or until an instant-read thermometer inserted into the thickest part of the thigh, away from the bone, registers 180°F; about 45 minutes before the turkey is done, remove the foil tent. Let the turkey stand, loosely covered with foil, for 20 minutes before carving.

Serves 8

A Fruit Garland for the Bird

Give your holiday bird a touch of glamour by serving it encircled by lush fruits in rich, Della Robbia colors. Fresh apricots, figs, pears, apples, star fruit, and sprigs of variegated sage will make your turkey, goose, or capon into a tabletop still life. For added drama, use a large-hole fruit zester or vegetable peeler to remove the peel from an orange or lemon in long strips. Wind the strips around a chopstick and let stand until the strips hold their curl. Use the strips to encircle the bird in ribbony spirals.

corn bread &
sausage stuffing

MAIN COURSES

tHIS IS INDEED THE STUFFING THAT YOU remember from your childhood and were always trying to re-create at home. Now you have the definitive recipe. Some like sausages hot, others like them sweet, but either kind will do just fine here.

I pound hot or sweet Italian sausage, casings removed

6 tablespoons (¾ stick) unsalted butter

3 celery stalks, finely chopped

I cup finely chopped onions

I ½ teaspoons ground sage

I teaspoon dried thyme

¾ teaspoon salt

¼ teaspoon freshly ground pepper, or more to taste

10 cups coarsely crumbled corn bread, dried out
   (see Note)

2 large eggs, beaten

I to 2 cups turkey or chicken stock or canned
   low-sodium chicken broth

1. Preheat the oven to 325°F. Butter a shallow 2-quart baking dish and set aside.

2. In a large skillet, cook the sausage over medium heat, stirring and breaking up any clumps of meat with a wooden spoon, until browned, about 10 minutes. Using a slotted spoon, transfer the sausage to a bowl. Drain off any fat from the skillet and wipe out the pan with paper towels.

3. Add the butter to the pan and melt over medium-high heat. Add the celery and onions and cook, stirring occasionally, until softened and translucent, about 10 minutes. Remove from the heat and stir in the sage, thyme, salt, and pepper.

4. Put the corn bread in a large bowl. Add the onion mixture, sausage, and beaten eggs and toss to mix well. Add enough stock to moisten the stuffing, stirring to combine. Transfer the stuffing to the prepared baking dish and drizzle about ¼ cup stock over the top. (The stuffing can be prepared ahead to this point, covered, and refrigerated for up to 6 hours. Add an extra 10 minutes or so to the baking time.)

5. Bake the stuffing for 35 to 40 minutes, or until golden brown on top and heated through.

Serves 8

 Note

Fresh corn bread can be air-dried or dried in the oven. Spread the crumbled corn bread on two large baking sheets and let stand overnight at room temperature to dry out. Or bake in a 350°F oven, stirring occasionally, for 30 minutes, or until dried but not browned.

Packaged corn bread stuffing mix is fine here, but omit the salt and pepper and perhaps the herbs (depending on the brand) listed in the recipe. Use corn bread made from a mix (an 11-ounce package will yield about 5 cups crumbled) only as a last resort.

couscous, raisin &
pistachio stuffing

IF YOU'RE PLANNING ON TUCKING AWAY ALL those homemade breadsticks at Thanksgiving dinner, you don't really need to add even more bread to the stuffing. Instead, this extremely flavorful Mediterranean-style side dish based on couscous will keep things interesting. It's heady with imported spices—and even boasts some tender pistachio nuts.

6 tablespoons olive oil

2 large onions, finely chopped

½ cup finely chopped celery with leaves

½ cup finely chopped carrot

2 garlic cloves, chopped

1 yellow or orange bell pepper, trimmed, seeded,
   and finely chopped

½ cup golden raisins

⅓ cup shelled pistachio nuts, toasted

¼ cup finely chopped fresh parsley

2 teaspoons ground coriander

1 teaspoon ground cumin

¼ teaspoon ground allspice

¼ teaspoon freshly ground pepper

3 cups chicken broth

½ teaspoon salt

One 10-ounce box (1⅔ cups) couscous

2 tablespoons unsalted butter, cut into bits

1. In a large skillet, heat 4 tablespoons of the oil over medium heat. Add the onions, celery, carrot, and garlic and cook, stirring occasionally, about 6 minutes, or until the vegetables are softened. Add the bell pepper and cook, stirring occasionally, for 3 minutes. Add the raisins, pistachios, parsley, coriander, cumin, allspice, and pepper and cook, stirring, for 1 minute. Transfer the mixture to a large bowl.

2. In a large saucepan, bring 2¼ cups broth, the remaining 2 tablespoons oil, and the salt to a boil over high heat. Remove the pan from the heat, stir in the couscous, and let stand covered for 5 minutes, or until the liquid is absorbed. Fluff the couscous with a fork, add it to the onion mixture, and combine gently and thoroughly.

3. Preheat the oven to 325°F. Generously butter a 3- to 4-quart baking dish.

4. Transfer the stuffing to the prepared baking dish, drizzle with the remaining ¾ cup broth, and dot with the butter. Cover tightly with foil and bake for 30 minutes. Remove the foil and bake, uncovered, for 30 minutes longer.

Serves 8 to 10

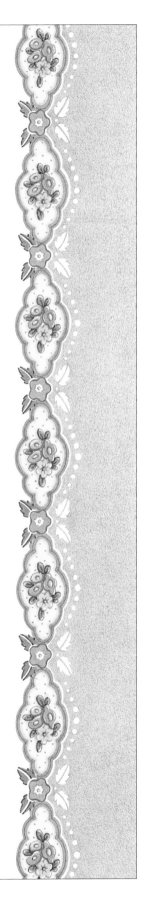

traditional

roasted goose

fOR A DICKENSIAN THANKSGIVING OR Christmas dinner this year, roast a goose with all the proper trimmings. We might have titled this recipe "Upside-down Goose," because that's exactly what you do: Steaming the goose renders its fat (goose is a high-fat bird), and after it's steamed, it's cooked breast side down to make it even moister.

One 12-pound goose

Salt and freshly ground pepper

4 tablespoons (½ stick) unsalted butter

6 small Golden Delicious apples, each peeled, cored, and cut into 8 wedges

3 tablespoons sugar

1 ½ teaspoons fresh thyme leaves or ½ teaspoon dried

¼ teaspoon ground allspice

Generous pinch of dried sage

1 ½ cups (8 ounces) pitted prunes, cut into quarters

½ cup brandy

2 tablespoons water

1. Rinse the goose inside and out and pat dry with paper towels. Remove the excess fat from the body and neck cavities (reserve it for another use, if desired). Using a sharp skewer or small sharp knife, prick the skin of the thighs and the lower part of the breast all over, without piercing the meat. Tuck the wings under the back of the goose and tie the legs together with kitchen string. Place a rack in a large roasting pan, set the pan over one or two stovetop burners, and add enough water to come to just under the rack, without touching. Place the goose, breast side up, on the rack and bring the water just to a simmer. Cover the pan tightly with a lid or foil and steam the goose for 45 minutes. If necessary, remove some of the liquid fat as it accumulates in the pan, using a bulb baster (be careful of the steam when you uncover the pan), or add additional water.

2. Preheat the oven to 325°F.

3. Transfer the goose to a platter and pour off the fat from the roasting pan (reserve it for another use, if desired.) Sprinkle the goose all over with salt and pepper to taste and place, breast side down, on the rack in the roasting pan. Roast for 1 ¼ hours, then turn the goose over and roast for 45 minutes to 1 hour longer, until an instant-read thermometer inserted into the thickest part of the thigh, away from the bone, registers 175° to 180°F. Remove the goose from the oven, transfer to a cutting board, and let the goose stand, loosely covered with foil, for 15 minutes before carving.

4. Meanwhile, melt the butter in a large deep skillet over medium-high heat. Add the apple, sprinkle with the sugar, thyme, allspice, sage, and ⅛ teaspoon salt, and cook, stirring frequently, until the apples are tender and slightly caramelized, 12 to 15 minutes.

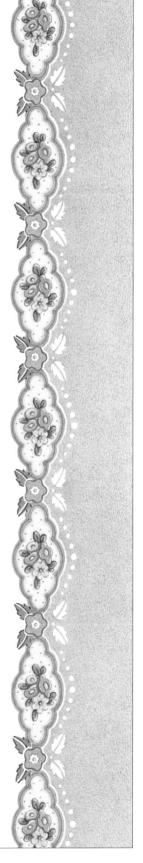

5. While the apples are cooking, in a medium saucepan, combine the prunes and brandy and bring to a simmer over low heat. Simmer, stirring occasionally, until the prunes are soft and most of the liquid has been absorbed, 5 to 7 minutes.

6. Add the prunes and the water to the apples and stir well with a wooden spoon, scraping up any caramelized bits from the bottom of the pan. Serve with the carved goose.

Serves 8

mediterranean
filet mignon

hERE IS A RICH DISH FOR GOOD FRIENDS, perfect for serving on a cozy New Year's Eve, when memories unfold. The earthy flavors of olives and sun-dried tomatoes might even inspire you to reminisce about your trip to Italy.

> Eight 1-inch-thick (4 to 5 ounces each)
>   filets mignons
> ½ teaspoon salt
> ¼ teaspoon freshly ground pepper
> 2 tablespoons olive oil
> 2 cups chicken broth
> ½ cup pitted Mediterranean-style black
>   olives, chopped
> ½ cup drained sun-dried tomatoes,
>   chopped
> ¼ cup minced fresh parsley

1. Sprinkle the filets with the salt and pepper. In a large heavy skillet, heat the oil over medium-high heat until hot but not smoking. Add the filets and cook for about 5 minutes on each side for medium-rare. With tongs, transfer the filets to a warmed plate, cover with foil, and keep warm.

2. Add the broth, olives, sun-dried tomatoes, and 2 tablespoons of the parsley to the skillet. Bring mixture to a boil over medium-high heat and cook for 3 to 5 minutes, until thickened. Carefully stir in any accumulated juices from the meat.

3. Transfer the filets to serving plates, top with the pan sauce, and sprinkle with the remaining 2 tablespoons parsley.

Serves 8

Creating a Memorable Menu

In early November, start planning your holiday meals. Try to create a balanced mix of vegetarian, meat, seafood, and poultry dishes. Resolve to try something new—perhaps serving capon or duck instead of the usual roasted turkey. Desserts should be just as varied—they're the last thing you savor at a meal, and many times the most memorable part. Try to mix the usual chocolaty cake fare with lighter, fresher fruit-based treats, including sorbets, puddings, mousses, and ice creams. Traditional at Christmas too, is a large wheel of Stilton, which should be set out with rounds of toast, fresh bread, crunchy crackers and surrounded by seedless grapes or sliced apples.

shiitake & sage-scented

pot roast

gIVE CHANUKKAH DINNERS A NEW TWIST this year: Grandmother might not even recognize her favorite pot roast, updated here with shiitake mushrooms and slow-roasted with wine and herbs. Don't despair if you can't find the shiitakes—good old white button mushrooms will do fine. To enhance the flavor, you may want to add ½ ounce dried porcinis or other dried mushrooms soaked in ¾ cup boiling water for 30 minutes. Just rinse the porcinis after soaking, strain the soaking liquid through cheesecloth, and mix them together along with the button mushrooms.

¼ cup vegetable oil

One 4-pound fresh beef brisket, trimmed

4 red onions, sliced

2 garlic cloves, thinly sliced

3 tablespoons all-purpose flour

1 pound fresh shiitake mushrooms, stems discarded

One 13¾- to 14½-ounce can beef broth

1¼ cups dry red wine

¼ cup chopped fresh parsley

4 large fresh sage leaves

1 bay leaf

1½ teaspoons fresh thyme leaves

½ teaspoon salt

¼ teaspoon freshly ground pepper

1. Preheat the oven to 325°F.

2. In a large Dutch oven, heat the oil over medium-high heat. Add the brisket and brown on all sides, about 10 minutes. With tongs, transfer the brisket to a plate and set aside.

3. Reduce the heat to medium and add the onions. Cook, stirring occasionally, for 15 minutes, or until lightly browned. Add the garlic and cook, stirring, for 30 seconds. Stir in the flour and cook, stirring, for 2 minutes, or until lightly browned.

4. Return the brisket to the Dutch oven. Stir in the mushrooms, broth, red wine, 2 tablespoons parsley, sage, bay leaf, thyme leaves, salt, and pepper and bring to a boil over high heat. Cover, transfer to the oven, and cook for 2½ hours, or until the brisket is fork tender.

5. Transfer the meat from the Dutch oven to a cutting board and let it rest, loosely covered with foil, for 15 minutes. Skim the fat from the sauce. Discard the sage and bay leaves. Bring the sauce to a boil over high heat, reduce the heat to medium-high, and cook, stirring occasionally, for 15 minutes, or until the sauce is slightly thickened. Stir in the remaining 2 tablespoons of the parsley. Transfer the sauce to a sauceboat.

6. Slice the pot roast across the grain, arrange on a large serving platter, and serve with the sauce.

Serves 8 to 10

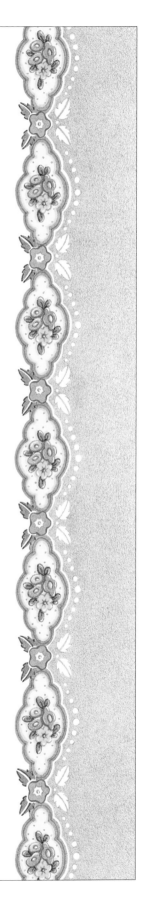

peppered beef tenderloin

rOAST TENDERLOIN IS UTTERLY SIMPLE TO prepare, yet elegant enough for a New Year's Eve celebration. You can prepare both the spice mix and the horseradish cream ahead of time, leaving very little to be done at the last minute.

I tablespoon black peppercorns

I tablespoon white peppercorns

I tablespoons coriander seeds

¾ teaspoon salt

One 3-pound beef tenderloin roast

About 1 ½ teaspoons vegetable oil

¾ cup heavy cream

3 tablespoons drained bottled white horseradish

Freshly ground pepper, to taste

1. Preheat the oven to 425°F. Lightly oil a roasting pan.

2. Combine the peppercorns and coriander seeds in a spice grinder or clean coffee grinder and coarsely grind them. (You can also use a mortar and pestle to grind the spices or a pepper mill set on its coarsest grind.) Combine the salt with the ground spices and blend well.

3. Rub the beef all over with the oil and then rub the spice mixture evenly over the meat. Place the roast in the prepared roasting pan and roast for 25 to 30 minutes for rare (an instant-read thermometer should read about 125°F) or 30 to 35 minutes for medium-rare (130° to 135°F.)

4. Meanwhile, in a medium bowl, beat the cream with an electric mixer until soft peaks form. With a rubber spatula, fold in the horseradish. Season with pepper. Cover and refrigerate until ready to serve. (The cream can be prepared up to 4 hours in advance; if necessary, whisk gently back to soft peaks before serving.)

5. Transfer the roast to a cutting board, preferably one with a "moat" for juices. Let stand for 10 minutes before slicing. Serve with the horseradish cream.

Serves 8

classic yorkshire pudding with
standing rib roast

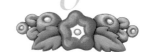

STANDING RIB ROAST IMMEDIATELY SIGNALS an important occasion. Yorkshire pudding, by the way, isn't a dessert: It's more of a popover made from beef drippings that you eat with a knife and fork.

RIB ROAST & GRAVY

1 standing rib roast (about 10 pounds), chine bone removed

Salt and freshly ground pepper, to taste

¼ cup all-purpose flour

1 cup beef broth

1 cup water

2 tablespoons unsalted butter, at room temperature

2 tablespoons heavy cream

YORKSHIRE PUDDING

⅓ cup beef drippings plus additional for muffin pan

1 cup all-purpose flour

Pinch of salt

2 large eggs

⅔ cup water

⅔ cup milk

1 shallot, minced

1 garlic clove, minced

1 tablespoon minced fresh flat-leaf parsley

1. Make the rib roast and gravy. Preheat the oven to 425°F. Place the beef on a rack in a large roasting pan, season with salt and pepper, and roast for 30 minutes. Reduce the heat to 325°F and roast until an instant-read thermometer inserted in the thickest part of the meat, away from the bone, registers 125°F for rare or 140°F for medium. Transfer to a cutting board, cover loosely with foil, and let rest for 15 minutes.

2. Pour ¼ cup of the drippings from the roasting pan into a small saucepan; heat over medium heat, then gradually whisk in the flour. Cook, whisking constantly, for about 2 minutes. Add the broth and water and boil, whisking constantly, until slightly thickened. Remove the saucepan from the heat and stir in the butter and cream. Season with salt and pepper.

3. Meanwhile, make the Yorkshire pudding. Increase the oven temperature to 425°F. Coat 12 muffin cups with drippings.

4. In the bowl of a food processor, combine the flour, salt, eggs, water, milk, and 2 tablespoons beef drippings; process just until blended. Let stand at room temperature for 15 minutes.

5. Meanwhile, in a small skillet, heat the remaining beef drippings over medium-high heat. Add the shallot and garlic and cook, stirring frequently, for 3 minutes, or until softened.

6. Stir the cooked shallot mixture and the parsley into the batter. Fill the prepared muffin cups two-thirds full with batter and bake for 15 minutes. Reduce the heat to 375°F and bake for 15 minutes, or until puffed and golden brown.

7. Carve the rib roast and arrange on serving plates. Pour the pan gravy into a sauceboat and serve with the roast.

Serves 8

moroccan-spiced pork loin

WITH ITS MOROCCAN-INSPIRED RUB OF fragrant spices—cumin, coriander, cardamom, and anise seeds—this succulent pork roast doesn't even really need any other adornment. But if you want to dress it up, serve our made-in-minutes orange sauce, laced with some of the same spices, alongside. Cardamom adds a subtle, almost musky flavor, but you can omit it if necessary.

PORK ROAST

2 large garlic cloves, finely minced

1 ½ teaspoons cumin seeds, lightly crushed

1 teaspoon ground coriander

1 teaspoon ground cardamom

½ teaspoon anise or fennel seeds, lightly crushed

2 tablespoons olive oil

One 4-pound boneless center-cut pork loin roast, trimmed of excess fat

Salt and freshly ground pepper, to taste

ORANGE SAUCE

1 cup orange marmalade

2 tablespoons dry white wine

2 tablespoons water

½ teaspoon ground coriander

⅜ teaspoon paprika, or more to taste

¼ teaspoon ground cardamom, or to taste

Pinch of salt

1. Make the pork roast. Combine the garlic, cumin seeds, coriander, cardamom, anise seeds, and oil in a small cup and mix well. Lightly oil a small roasting pan and put the pork roast in the pan. Rub the spice mixture all over the meat, turn the roast fat side up, and let marinate at room temperature for 30 minutes to 1 hour.

2. Preheat the oven to 450°F.

3. Season the pork generously with salt and pepper. Roast for 15 minutes. Reduce the oven temperature to 325°F and roast for 45 to 60 minutes longer (depending on the thickness of the roast), or until an instant-read thermometer inserted into the center of the meat registers 145° to 150°F. Transfer the pork to a cutting board and let rest for 15 minutes. (The internal temperature of the meat will rise to about 155°F.)

4. Meanwhile, make the orange sauce. In a small saucepan, combine the marmalade, wine, water, coriander, paprika, cardamom, and salt and bring to a boil over medium heat, stirring occasionally. Remove from the heat and let cool to room temperature. (The sauce can be made several hours ahead, covered with plastic wrap, and refrigerated.)

5. To serve, thinly slice the pork, arrange on a serving platter, and serve with the sauce on the side.

Serves 8

dried cherry–stuffed
loin of pork

MAIN COURSES

P LAY UP THE SWEETNESS OF THIS SUCCU-
lent pork loin stuffed with dried cherries by
serving it with a beet or carrot side dish from
Chapter Four, such as Fresh Ginger-Sauteed Baby
Carrots (page 79). If the pork loin dwarfs your roasting pan,
just cut it in half crosswise and roast it in two pieces. To test
for doneness, be sure to check the temperature by inserting
the thermometer into the meat, not the stuffing!

DRIED CHERRY-STUFFED
LOIN OF PORK

2 tablespoons olive oil

I small red onion, finely chopped

2 garlic cloves, minced

2 teaspoons fresh thyme leaves, plus additional
sprigs for garnish

¼ cup water

½ cup golden raisins

½ cup dried sour cherries or cranberries

½ teaspoon salt

½ teaspoon freshly ground pepper

One 4- to 4½-pound boneless center-cut
pork loin, butterflied and trimmed of
fat, at room temperature

I ½ teaspoons ground allspice

PAN GRAVY

2 ½ cups chicken broth or water

¼ cup golden raisins

Pinch of salt

Pinch of freshly ground pepper

1. Make the dried cherry–stuffed loin of pork. In a medium
saucepan, heat the oil over medium heat. Add the onion, garlic, and thyme and cook, stirring frequently, for 5 minutes, or
until the onion is softened.

2. Add the water and bring the mixture to a boil over high
heat. Add the raisins, dried cherries, ¼ teaspoon each salt and
pepper, and stir to combine well. Remove the pan from the
heat, cover tightly, and let steep for 10 minutes. Transfer to a
bowl and let cool completely. Cover tightly with plastic wrap
and set aside.

3. Preheat the oven to 325°F.

4. On a clean work surface, lay the pork loin out flat,
trimmed side down, with one long side facing you. Sprinkle
evenly with the remaining ¼ teaspoon each salt and pepper
and the allspice.

5. Spoon the cooled fruit mixture onto the pork loin in a
2-inch-thick line, placed about 2 inches from the edge closest
to you, and 1½ inches from the edge of each short side.
Beginning with the long edge closest to you, roll up the pork

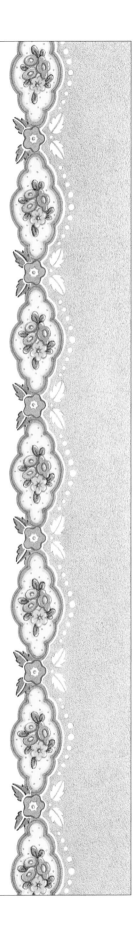

loin tightly into a long cylinder. With kitchen string, tie the pork loin crosswise at 1-inch intervals.

6. Place the pork loin on a large wire rack in a large roasting pan. Roast the pork loin for 1½ hours, or until an instant-read thermometer registers 145°F.

7. Remove the pork loin from the oven, reserving the roasting pan and the juices for the gravy. Transfer the pork loin to a cutting board and cover with foil to keep warm. Let the pork loin stand for 10 minutes before cutting.

8. Meanwhile, make the pan gravy. Remove the rack from the roasting pan. Spoon off and discard all but 1 tablespoon of the fat from the drippings in the pan. Place the pan directly on the stovetop and add the chicken broth and raisins. Bring the mixture to a boil over high heat, scraping the pan with a wooden spoon to loosen any browned bits. Boil for 10 minutes or until the liquid is reduced. Stir in the salt and pepper, and strain into a gravy boat.

9. To serve, remove the kitchen string from the pork loin and, with a carving knife, cut the roast crosswise into ½-inch-thick slices. Garnish with the thyme sprigs and serve the pan gravy on the side.

Serves 8

A Child's Christmas

- Let children be the designated greeters for holiday guests at the door. Have them hand each one a small wrapped gift.

- Start a collection of holiday cookie cutters in shapes such as turkeys, pumpkins, stars, candles, reindeer, and Christmas trees. Make cookies with the kids and eat them fresh out of the oven. Or throw a family bakeathon the first or second week of December. Freeze multiple batches of each person's favorite cookies.

- Set a kids' holiday table with all the trimmings. Cover the children's table with white craft paper and supply crayons for decorating. For the centerpiece, fill a bowl with gingerbread cookies, each decorated a little differently. Give each child a peppermint stick to stir hot cocoa.

peach compote with bourbon- *glazed ham*

MAIN COURSES

i F YOU HAVE ANY SOUTHERN BLOOD, Y'ALL know about how sweet fruit sauces enhance meats. In this case, a gingered peach compote perfectly complements the salty ham. For real good luck there's no better dish to serve with The Classic Hoppin' John (page 63) on New Year's Day.

GINGER-PEACH COMPOTE

One 20-ounce bag frozen unsweetened peaches, partially thawed and coarsely chopped

3 tablespoons light brown sugar

1 ½ tablespoons finely minced peeled ginger

¼ teaspoon ground ginger

3 tablespoons orange juice

BOURBON-GLAZED HAM

½ cup bourbon

½ cup packed dark brown sugar

One 5- to 6-pound smoked ham

1. Preheat the oven to 325°F.

2. Make the ginger-peach compote. In a large heavy saucepan, combine the peaches, brown sugar, fresh ginger, ground ginger, and orange juice. Bring to a simmer over medium heat, stirring occasionally. Reduce the heat and simmer, stirring occasionally, until the peaches are tender but not mushy, 25 to 30 minutes.

3. Transfer the peach mixture to a bowl and let cool slightly. Cover with plastic wrap and refrigerate until cold. (The compote can be made up to 1 day ahead.)

4. Meanwhile, make the bourbon-glazed ham. In a cup, combine the bourbon and brown sugar, stirring to dissolve the sugar. Set the bourbon glaze aside.

5. Place the ham, fat side up, in a shallow roasting pan. Cover tightly with foil and bake until an instant-read thermometer inserted into the thickest part of the ham, away from the bone, registers 140°F, about 1½ hours (or bake the ham according to the package directions). Twenty to 30 minutes before the ham is done, remove the foil and brush the ham generously with the bourbon glaze; continue to bake uncovered, brushing 2 or 3 more times with the remaining glaze. Transfer the ham to a platter and let rest for 15 minutes before carving and serving.

6. Carve the ham and serve with the peach compote in a bowl on the side.

Serves 8

rosemary-rubbed roasted
fresh ham

MAIN COURSES

HOLD THE PINEAPPLES! THIS RECIPE CALLS for fresh ham, which is quite different from smoked ham. In fact, you may need to order the ham ahead of time from your butcher. Keep in mind that rolled-and-tied leg of pork also goes by the alias "fresh ham." The rosemary marinade for this mouthwatering ham gives it a distinctive flavor all its own. If the family is planning to watch winter sports together, use the leftovers to make delicious sandwiches with cranberry relish and crispy lettuce.

½ boneless leg of pork (fresh ham; 6 to 7

   pounds), preferably butt end, rolled

   and tied

4 large garlic cloves, minced

1 tablespoon dried rosemary, crumbled

2 tablespoons kosher salt

1 ½ teaspoons freshly ground pepper

1. The night before you want to serve the ham, untie the ham and, if necessary, trim off all but a thin layer of fat. In a small bowl, combine the garlic, rosemary, salt, and pepper. Rub the mixture all over the pork, inside and out. Place in a large roasting pan, cover with plastic wrap, and refrigerate overnight.

2. Preheat the oven to 425°F.

3. With a sharp knife, score the fat, and any skin, on the ham in a crosshatch pattern. With kitchen string, tie the ham back into its original shape. Place the ham, fatty side up, on a rack in another large roasting pan.

4. Roast the ham for 15 minutes. Cover the pan loosely with foil, reduce the oven temperature to 350°F, and roast for 2½ to 3 hours longer. Remove the foil for the last 30 minutes of cooking. Cook until an instant-read thermometer inserted into the thickest part of the meat registers 150°F.

5. Transfer the roast to a carving board, cover loosely, and let rest for 15 to 20 minutes before carving.

Serves 8

the classic
hoppin' john

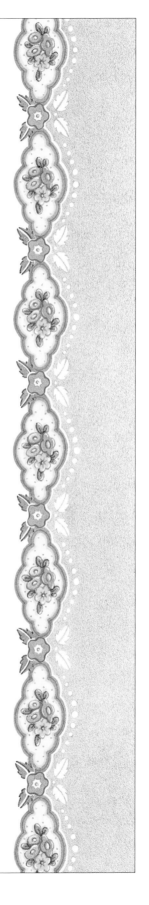

bEFORE THE PARTY STARTS ON NEW YEAR'S Eve, remember to put your black-eyed peas in water to soak overnight. The next day, get cooking early: Legend has it that this classic dish from the Deep South brings good luck if eaten on New Year's Day.

2 cups dried black-eyed peas, picked over
   and rinsed

8 cups cool water

1 smoked ham hock

2 onions, coarsely chopped

2 bay leaves

½ teaspoon dried thyme

¼ teaspoon ground red pepper

2 cups long-grain white rice

1 teaspoon salt

Chopped tomatoes, scallions, and fresh parsley,
   for garnish

1. In a large Dutch oven, soak the black-eyed peas in cool water to cover by 2 inches overnight. (Or quick-soak the peas: In a large Dutch oven, bring the peas and enough cool water to cover by 2 inches to a boil over medium heat. Boil for 2 minutes, remove from the heat, and let the peas stand, covered, for 1 hour.) In a colander, drain the peas. Rinse the Dutch oven.

2. In the Dutch oven, bring the water, ham hock, onions, bay leaves, thyme, and ground red pepper to a boil over high heat. Reduce the heat to low and simmer, covered, for 30 minutes.

3. Add the peas, return the mixture to a boil over high heat, and skim any scum from the surface. Reduce the heat and cook at a bare simmer for at least 1 hour, or until the peas are tender when pierced with a fork. Remove and discard the ham hock and bay leaves.

4. Add the rice and salt, making sure there is enough liquid to cover the rice. Stir gently, and simmer, covered, over low heat for 25 minutes, or until the rice is tender.

5. Serve the hoppin' john in bowls garnished with chopped tomatoes, scallions, and parsley.

Serves 8

fresh mint sauce &
roasted leg of lamb

I F ONLY ALL OF LIFE'S SUCCESSES COULD be so easy to accomplish as this one. Once you try the homemade green mint sauce, you will never go back to mint jelly again!

MAIN COURSES

FRESH MINT SAUCE

2 bunches fresh mint

½ cup plus 4 teaspoons cool water

½ cup sugar

I cup rice vinegar

I tablespoon cornstarch

Pinch of salt

I red onion, sliced

3 tablespoons olive oil

4 garlic cloves, peeled

4 sprigs fresh parsley

2 sprigs plus I teaspoon chopped fresh rosemary

2 sprigs plus I teaspoon chopped fresh thyme

One 7-pound bone-in leg of lamb, trimmed,
**   at room temperature**

½ teaspoon salt

¼ teaspoon freshly ground pepper

1. Make the fresh mint sauce. Discard the tough stems from 1 bunch of mint. In the bowl of a food processor, pulse the mint until coarsely chopped.

2. In a medium saucepan, bring ½ cup of the water and the sugar to a simmer over medium heat, stirring to dissolve the sugar. Add the vinegar and the chopped mint and bring the mixture to a boil over medium-high heat.

3. Meanwhile, in a small bowl, stir together the remaining 4 teaspoons water, the cornstarch, and salt. Add to the vinegar mixture, bring to a boil over high heat, and boil for 1 minute, or until slightly thickened. Let the mixture stand for 30 minutes. Strain the sauce through a fine sieve and refrigerate, covered, until ready to serve.

4. Preheat the oven to 450°F. In the center of a large roasting pan, toss the onion with 1 tablespoon of the oil and the garlic. Place the parsley and rosemary and thyme sprigs on top. Arrange the lamb on top of the herb sprigs. Drizzle with the remaining 2 tablespoons oil and sprinkle with the chopped rosemary, thyme, salt, and pepper.

5. Roast the lamb for 15 minutes. Reduce oven temperature to 350°F and roast, basting every 15 minutes with pan juices, 1 to 1¼ hours, until an instant-read thermometer inserted into the thickest part of the meat, away from the bone, registers 145°F for medium-rare. Transfer the lamb to a cutting board and let it rest, loosely covered with foil, for 15 minutes.

6. Just before serving, chop ⅓ cup mint leaves from the remaining bunch of mint, add to the chilled mint sauce, and transfer the mixture to a serving bowl. Remove the kitchen string from the lamb, carve, arrange on a serving platter, and serve accompanied by the fresh mint sauce.

Serves 8

rosemary-roasted
rack of lamb

t HE KIDS ARE HOME ON CHRISTMAS break. Aunt Edna and Uncle Bud said they might drop by. Time to break out the celebration foods. If you can't get large 8-rib racks (each weighing about 1¾ pounds, trimmed), substitute three smaller 7-rib racks.

2 large 8-rib racks of lamb, trimmed and frenched (have the butcher do this)

6 garlic cloves, halved and smashed

3 tablespoons finely chopped fresh rosemary or 1 ½ tablespoons crumbled dried

1 tablespoon olive oil

Salt and freshly ground pepper

1. Place the lamb in a large baking dish or shallow bowl. Combine the garlic, rosemary, and oil in a small cup and rub all over the lamb. Cover and refrigerate for at least 2 hours. (The lamb can be kept refrigerated for up to 8 hours.)

2. Preheat the oven to 450°F.

3. Remove the lamb and brush off any garlic. Season the racks generously on both sides with salt and pepper. Place the racks, fat side up, in a shallow roasting pan. Roast for 25 to 30 minutes, until an instant-read thermometer inserted in the center of the lamb, away from the bone, registers 140°F for medium-rare. Let stand for 10 minutes before carving into individual chops.

Serves 8

Sharing Hospitality—and Chores—with Friends

Plan a progressive dinner with a group of neighbors. Each family prepares just one course. Not only are the cooking chores divided up, but you get to see each others' holiday-decorated houses!

Alternatively, form a "supper club" with a group of friends. Choose a different theme each week, such as Christmas in Barcelona, Kwanzaa, or Chanukkah in Israel, and have each member contribute a single dish appropriate for the festival. Leave it to the host family to provide thematic decorations, and divide the menu and beverages among the other guests. Not only do you lighten the load of cooking a holiday meal, but you actually learn something about different cultures and traditions.

shrimp &
sausage gumbo

gUMBO IS ACTUALLY A CREOLIZATION OF the African word *gombo*, which is another name for okra. Little wonder, then, that it suits Kwanzaa celebrations so well.

1 ½ cups trimmed and chopped fresh or thawed
    frozen okra

2 small red onions, sliced

4 inner celery stalks with leaves, sliced

¾ cup chopped yellow bell peppers

¾ cup minced fresh flat-leaf parsley

3 garlic cloves, thinly sliced

1 bay leaf

1 ½ teaspoons salt

¾ teaspoon freshly ground pepper

¾ teaspoon ground red pepper

¾ teaspoon dried thyme

¼ teaspoon ground allspice

1 pound cooked andouille or kielbasa sausage, halved
    lengthwise and sliced crosswise ½ inch thick

Vegetable oil

½ cup all-purpose flour

4 cups chicken broth

¼ cup tomato paste

1 ½ cups water

5 plum tomatoes, seeded and chopped

1 pound medium shrimp, shelled and deveined

½ cup minced scallion greens

2 tablespoons distilled white vinegar

Hot cooked white rice, for serving

1. In a large bowl, stir together the okra, onions, celery, bell peppers, ¼ cup of the parsley, the garlic, bay leaf, salt, pepper, ground red pepper, thyme, and allspice and combine well. Set the mixture aside.

2. In a large Dutch oven or large heavy pot, cook the sausage, stirring constantly, over medium heat for about 6 minutes, or until lightly browned. With a slotted spoon, transfer to a bowl. Pour the fat from the pan into a glass measure and add enough vegetable oil to measure ½ cup. Return the oil to the pot and heat over medium-low heat, scraping up any browned bits on the bottom of the pot. Gradually add the flour and cook, stirring frequently, for about 30 minutes, or until this roux is a very dark rich brown.

3. Immediately add the broth and scrape up any browned bits. Blend the tomato paste and water and add to the pot along with the vegetable mixture, the sausage, and tomatoes. Heat the mixture to boiling over high heat; reduce the heat to low and simmer for 1 hour, or until thick.

4. Stir in the shrimp, scallions, the remaining ½ cup parsley, and the vinegar. Remove the Dutch oven from the heat, cover, and let stand for 10 minutes. Remove and discard the bay leaf. Serve the gumbo in bowls with the rice.

Serves 8

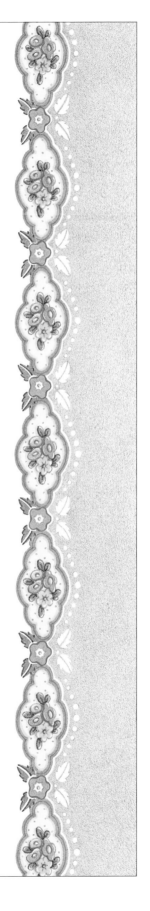

court bouillon–
poached redfish

r ED SNAPPER IS A TRADITIONAL CHRISTMAS Creole dish—the rosy color is so naturally festive. Now, it's become a staple of Kwanzaa celebrations, owing to Creole cookery's African roots. Traditionalists prepare the fish in this spicy dish whole, but our easier version uses fillets. Serve with plenty of hot cooked rice.

MAIN COURSES

2 tablespoons vegetable oil

2 tablespoons all-purpose flour

I large onion, finely chopped

2 garlic cloves, minced

I large celery stalk, finely chopped

I large bunch scallions, minced

I teaspoon fresh thyme leaves or generous
    ¼ teaspoon dried

Scant ¾ teaspoon ground allspice

2 bay leaves

One 28-ounce can whole tomatoes in juice,
    coarsely chopped

2 cups water

½ cup dry white or red wine

¾ teaspoon salt, or to taste

¼ teaspoon freshly ground pepper

½ to ¾ teaspoon ground red pepper

Eight 5-ounce red snapper fillets, left whole, or four
    9- to 10-ounce fillets, cut crosswise in half

I to 2 tablespoons fresh lemon juice

1. In a Dutch oven or large heavy pot, heat the oil over medium heat until hot. Stir in the flour and cook, stirring constantly, until the mixture is the color of peanut butter, 8 to 10 minutes.

2. Add the onion, garlic, celery, scallions, thyme, allspice, and bay leaves to the pot and stir well to combine. Add the tomatoes, water, wine, salt, pepper, and ground red pepper and bring to a boil over medium-high heat, stirring occasionally. Boil gently, stirring occasionally, until the sauce is slightly thickened, about 10 minutes.

3. Reduce the heat so the sauce is at a gentle simmer; if you are using whole fillets, transfer half of the sauce to a large deep skillet and bring just to a simmer. Place the fillets, skin side down, in the sauce, dividing them between the pans if necessary, and cook just until opaque throughout, 5 to 10 minutes, depending on the thickness of the fish; do not overcook. With a large slotted spatula, transfer the fish to a platter. Add the lemon juice to the sauce and adjust the seasoning, if necessary. Ladle the sauce over the fish on the platter, or arrange the fish in individual deep serving plates and spoon the sauce over each portion.

Serves 8

tomato & feta
greek shrimp

IMAGINE COMING BACK FROM AN AFTER-noon of sledding or an evening of caroling to this reward: appealingly pink sweet shrimp with a thin layer of tangy feta on top, all in an oniony tomato sauce. Though shrimp and cheese are admittedly an unusual combination, the flavor of the feta works in perfect harmony with the garlicky shrimp. Serve with plenty of hot rice and crusty bread.

3 tablespoons olive oil

4 onions, halved lengthwise and thinly sliced

3 garlic cloves, minced

Two 28-ounce cans diced tomatoes

½ cup dry white wine

1 ½ teaspoons dried oregano, crumbled

1 teaspoon salt, or to taste

⅜ teaspoon freshly ground pepper

½ cup finely chopped fresh flat-leaf parsley

2 ½ pounds medium to large shrimp, peeled and deveined

8 to 10 ounces good-quality feta cheese, cut into ¼-inch-thick slices

1. In a Dutch oven or large heavy pot, heat the oil over medium-high heat. Add the onions and cook, stirring frequently, until translucent, about 10 minutes; do not let brown. Add the garlic and cook, stirring, just until fragrant, 30 seconds to 1 minute.

2. Stir in the tomatoes, wine, oregano, salt, and pepper and bring to a simmer. Reduce the heat and simmer gently until the tomatoes are soft and the sauce has thickened, 15 to 20 minutes. (The sauce can be prepared ahead to this point and set aside, covered with plastic wrap, at room temperature, for up to 1 hour, or refrigerated for up to 6 hours; bring to a simmer before proceeding.)

3. Stir in the parsley, then add the shrimp, stirring them into the sauce. Lay the feta over the top, cover, and cook until the shrimp are pink and opaque throughout and the feta is melting, 12 to 15 minutes longer. Serve directly from the pot, or on individual dinner plates, making sure to spoon out all the juices from the pot.

Serves 8

Chapter Four

vegetables & side dishes

THE QUEEN OF THE KITCHEN

pepper-crusted
acorn squash

t HE WORD KWANZAA COMES FROM A PHRASE that means "first fruits." The holiday was patterned after the harvest festivals of Africa, and harvest fruits and vegetables are, naturally, important symbols. This tasty acorn squash dish perfectly suits the spirit of the celebration. Use a "gourmet" blend of pepper (black, white, green, and/or pink) if you have it.

3 large acorn squash, scrubbed

¼ cup (½ stick) unsalted butter, melted

Salt, to taste

1 teaspoon freshly ground pepper, preferably a peppercorn mix

1. Preheat the oven to 400°F. Lightly butter two large heavy baking sheets.

2. With a large sharp knife, cut each squash lengthwise in half (make sure the cutting board is securely anchored; it can be difficult to cut though the tough skin). Scrape out the seeds and strings, then cut crosswise into ½-inch-thick slices.

3. Arrange the squash slices in a single layer on the prepared baking sheets and brush with half the melted butter. Sprinkle generously with salt and then with half of the pepper. Bake for 15 minutes, then turn the squash and brush with the remaining melted butter. Sprinkle with salt and the remaining half of the pepper and bake for 10 to 15 minutes longer, or until the squash is tender. (The squash can be prepared to this point up to 2 hours ahead of time. Set aside, loosely covered, on the baking sheets, then reheat, uncovered, in a hot oven (325°F to 375°F, depending on what else you are cooking) for about 10 minutes.) Transfer to a serving plate and serve hot.

Serves 8

VEGETABLES &
SIDE DISHES

walnut-scented
roasted asparagus

WHEN YOU CRAVE THE TASTE OF NUTS but not the trouble of the nutcracker, this side dish should satisfy your urges. Richly flavored, aromatic walnut, hazelnut, and other nut oils should be purchased in small bottles, as they tend to go rancid quickly.

> 3 pounds asparagus, tough ends trimmed
>
> 2 tablespoons olive oil
>
> Salt and freshly ground pepper, to taste
>
> 2 to 3 ounces Parmesan cheese,
> sliced into thin shavings with a
> vegetable peeler
>
> 1 tablespoon walnut or other nut oil

1. Preheat the oven to 500°F.

2. Divide the asparagus between two large baking sheets, drizzle with the olive oil, and toss to coat. Spread the asparagus out and season generously with salt and pepper. Roast for 8 to 10 minutes (depending on the thickness of the asparagus), or until tender. Scatter the shaved cheese over the asparagus and return to the oven for about 2 minutes, or until the cheese begins to melt.

3. Transfer the asparagus to a serving platter or individual plates, drizzle with walnut oil, and serve immediately.

Serves 8

Festive Family Tables

Since it's only once a year:

- Use pinecones to hold place cards. Have some fun by omitting names and instead using photos of the particular person.

- Fill a glass hurricane with acorns, pecans, and tiny pumpkins for a centerpiece.

- Place an ornament at each table setting.

- Decorate the backs of chairs with colorful ribbons or miniature stockings.

- Select an interesting container and fill it with florist's foam. Trim and spray-paint greenery as desired, and insert cut ends into foam. Cover foam with moss.

- Make a glass tabletop tree using footed cake plates and candy dishes. Fill each tier with ornaments, greens, and small gifts.

- Tie each napkin in a sheer ribbon and tuck scented geranium leaves into the ribbons.

roasted beets &

onions

fOR THE RICHEST, MOST FLAVORFUL BEETS, look for those that still have their green tops attached (you can cook the greens as you would spinach.) Roasted in their jackets, beets take on a smoky flavor, as if they were cooked on a wood-burning stove. For a pleasing presentation, choose onions approximately the same size as the beets.

VEGETABLES & SIDE DISHES

8 small beets, trimmed to 1-inch stems, unpeeled

3 small red onions, unpeeled

3 tablespoons olive oil

½ cup chicken broth

¼ cup balsamic vinegar

1 ½ teaspoons fresh thyme leaves

¼ teaspoon salt

⅛ teaspoon freshly ground pepper

1. Preheat the oven to 400°F.

2. In a large cast-iron or other heavy skillet, toss the beets and red onions with the oil. Roast the vegetables, shaking the pan occasionally, for at least 1 hour and 15 minutes, until the onions are soft when pressed on and a fork will easily pierce the beets. You may need to leave the beets in a little longer than the onions, depending on their size.

3. Transfer the vegetables to a platter to cool. Place the skillet over high heat and bring the broth, vinegar, and 1 teaspoon of thyme to a boil. Cook, scraping with a wooden spoon to loosen any browned bits in the bottom of the pan, for about 4 minutes, until the liquid is dark, glossy brown, and syrupy. Add the salt and pepper.

4. When cool enough to handle, peel the beets and onions. Cut the beets into julienne strips and the onions into thin rings. Transfer to a large bowl, spoon the liquid over the onions and beets, add the remaining ½ teaspoon thyme leaves, and stir to combine. Transfer to a serving bowl and serve warm or at room temperature.

Serves 8

roasted red
peppers & broccoli

HOLIDAY REDS AND GREENS—THE COLORS of this dish—dance about in a side dish of broccoli florets with roasted red peppers. Adding a few jolly red Santas and miniature ornaments to the table, just for the fun of it, makes the dish even more celebratory. These colors aren't just appropriate for Christmas. During the African-American celebration of Kwanzaa, the kinara, a seven-branched candlestick, holds red, green, and black candles that are lit each evening. If you haven't got freshly roasted peppers, substitute a twelve-ounce jar of roasted red peppers, rinsed and drained.

2 roasted red bell peppers

2 bunches broccoli, trimmed and separated into
    2-inch florets

2 tablespoons olive oil

1 garlic clove, minced

½ teaspoon salt

Pinch of freshly ground pepper

1. On a cutting board, trim off the tops and bottoms of the roasted bell peppers; remove the seeds. Peel the peppers and cut them into ½-inch pieces. Set aside.

2. In a large pot of boiling salted water, cook the broccoli for 3 minutes, or until crisp-tender. Drain in a colander, refresh under cold running water to stop the cooking, drain again, and dry on paper towels.

3. In a large nonstick skillet, heat the oil over medium-high heat. Add the garlic and cook, stirring constantly, for 30 seconds. Add the broccoli, peppers, salt, and pepper and cook, stirring, for 2 minutes, or until heated through. Serve hot or at room temperature.

Serves 8

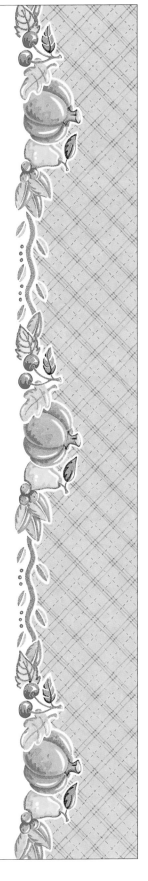

brussels sprouts
stir-fry

WHEN DID YOU LAST EAT BRUSSELS SPROUTS? Probably not for a while—and you've been missing out! The secret is to not overcook them, but to bring out their nutty taste. When buying them, look for heads that are tight and bright green. The littlest ones make the tastiest eating. Combined with sweet carrots and red peppers, they make a fortifying winter dish.

VEGETABLES &
SIDE DISHES

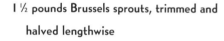

1 ½ pounds Brussels sprouts, trimmed and
   halved lengthwise

2 cups small cauliflower florets

4 slender carrots, peeled and cut into
   ¼-inch-thick slices

¼ cup vegetable oil

4 shallots, finely chopped

⅔ cup (¼-inch dice) red bell pepper

⅔ cup (¼-inch-thick shreds) red cabbage

½ cup water

¼ teaspoon salt

⅛ teaspoon freshly ground pepper

1. In a large saucepan of boiling salted water, cook the Brussels sprouts and the cauliflower for 4 minutes. Add the carrots and cook for 1 minute. Drain in a colander and refresh under cold water. Pat the vegetables dry on paper towels. Set aside.

2. In a large skillet, heat the oil over medium-high heat. Add the shallots and cook, stirring, for 1 minute. Stir in the bell pepper, cabbage, and the blanched vegetables. Stir-fry for 2 minutes. Add the water, salt, and pepper and cook for 3 to 5 minutes, until crisp-tender. Transfer to a serving bowl.

Serves 8

glazed
brussels sprouts

SURE, YOU COULD SERVE BRUSSELS SPROUTS with an elaborate béchamel or hollandaise sauce, but this method is a European classic. Just a dab of butter and a sprinkling of minced sweet shallots bring out their delicate taste. They make a perfect understated accompaniment for ham, roasted pork, or turkey.

2 pounds Brussels sprouts

3 to 4 tablespoons unsalted butter

⅔ cup thinly sliced shallots

¾ teaspoon salt, or more to taste

⅛ teaspoon freshly ground pepper

1. Bring a large pot of salted water to a boil. Meanwhile, trim the bottoms of the Brussels sprouts and remove any shriveled or discolored leaves. Cut the sprouts in half lengthwise, or into quarters if large.

2. Add the sprouts to the boiling water and cook just until tender and bright green, 3 to 5 minutes; drain immediately. (The sprouts can be prepared ahead to this point, cooled, covered, and refrigerated.)

3. In a large deep skillet, melt the butter over medium-high heat. Add the shallots and cook, stirring, until translucent, 3 to 5 minutes. Add the Brussels sprouts, salt, and pepper and cook, stirring, until heated through and just beginning to brown slightly, about 3 minutes. Serve hot.

Serves 8

Speaking of Side Dishes . . .

When planning a big holiday meal, your thoughts go straight to the entrée. But it's the side dishes that keep things interesting. In planning them, keep the following in mind:

- Chutneys and relishes cut the fat and richness of meat and game.

- Take your cue from the main course: Balance assertive tastes with those that are mild; for instance, if your main course is highly seasoned, go with a less complex side dish. At the same time, if you're serving a delicate fish, you don't want to overpower the taste with a spicy side dish.

- Create juxtapositions of textures: crunchy with soft, cooked with raw, succulent with crisp, hot with cold.

- One starchy dish—potatoes, rice, pasta, beans, or corn—is enough.

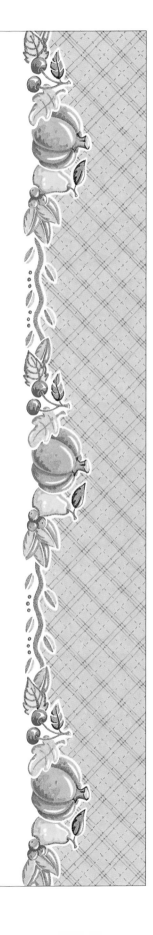

sweet & sour braised
red cabbage

WE LIKE THIS DISH WITH POT ROAST ON Chanukkah, but you'll savor its slow-cooked taste all winter long.

2 small heads red cabbage

3 tablespoons vegetable oil

2 red onions, finely chopped

1 Granny Smith apple, peeled, cored, and
   finely chopped

1 garlic clove, minced

One 13¾- to 14½-ounce can beef broth

1 cup apple juice

⅓ cup apple cider vinegar

¼ cup packed brown sugar

1 bay leaf

¾ teaspoon salt

¼ teaspoon freshly ground pepper

⅛ teaspoon ground allspice

1. With a sharp knife, cut each head of cabbage into quarters through the core. Remove and discard the cores. Discard the tough outer ribs of the cabbage and cut it into ¼-inch-thick slices.

2. In a Dutch oven, heat the oil over medium heat. Add the onions, apple, and garlic and cook, stirring, for 10 minutes, or until the onions are softened.

3. Stir in the cabbage, broth, apple juice, vinegar, sugar, bay leaf, salt, pepper, and allspice. Bring to a boil over high heat, reduce the heat to low, cover, and simmer, stirring occasionally, for 1¼ hours, or until the cabbage is very tender. Remove the cover and cook over medium-high heat, stirring occasionally, for 10 minutes longer, or until most of the liquid has evaporated. Remove and discard the bay leaf. Transfer the cabbage to a serving dish.

Serves 8

fresh ginger–sauteed
baby carrots

W E'RE GIVING "FAST FOOD" A NEW DEFINI-
tion with this dish, ready in seconds if you use
those peeled baby carrots from the supermarket.
Tossed with butter and kissed by ginger, it'll brighten
up any holiday meal.

Two 1-pound bags peeled baby carrots

3 tablespoons unsalted butter

2 tablespoons grated peeled ginger

Salt, to taste

¼ teaspoon freshly ground pepper

1. In a large pot of boiling salted water, cook the carrots until
just tender, 8 to 10 minutes. Drain thoroughly. (The carrots
can be prepared ahead to this point, covered and refrigerated.)

2. In a large skillet, melt the butter over medium heat. Add the
ginger, then the carrots, tossing to coat. Season with salt, add
the pepper, and heat, stirring frequently, until hot. Transfer to
a serving plate and serve immediately.

Serves 8

◆ Fresh Garlic–Sauteed Baby Carrots

For a more conventional sauteed carrot combination,
replace the freshly grated ginger with 2 or 3 minced garlic
cloves. Add the garlic to the butter and proceed with the
recipe. If you wish, replace the ground pepper with freshly
grated nutmeg.

cranberry *sauce*

CRANBERRY SAUCE IS AN ALL-AMERICAN classic—right up there with apple pie and white picket fences. It's easy to see why, too: Few dishes are so simply delicious, easy to make, and versatile. For a Southwestern variation, try stirring in ¼ cup of storebought hot pepper jelly after cooking. Make another plain batch just for the kids.

½ cup granulated sugar

¼ cup packed light brown sugar

¼ cup water

One 12-ounce bag fresh or thawed frozen cranberries, picked over and rinsed

Pinch of salt

1. In a medium saucepan, combine all of the ingredients. Bring to a boil over high heat, stirring occasionally. Reduce the heat to medium and cook, stirring occasionally, for 5 minutes, or until most of the cranberries pop and the mixture thickens slightly. Remove the saucepan from the heat.

2. Transfer the mixture to a serving bowl and cool to room temperature. Store, covered and chilled, until ready to serve.

Makes 2 cups

cranberry-orange *relish*

hERE ARE CRANBERRIES FOR GROWNUPS, with a splash of citrusy liqueur and bursts of fresh orange. Try tangelos for their tart mandarin taste or deep orange temples for intense sweetness.

One 12-ounce bag fresh or thawed frozen cranberries, picked over and rinsed

1 large orange, rinsed, cut into 12 chunks, including peel, and seeded

¾ cup sugar, or to taste

1 tablespoon Grand Marnier or other orange-flavored liqueur (optional)

1. In the bowl of a food processor, combine the cranberries and orange chunks and pulse until finely chopped. Transfer to a bowl and stir in the sugar and Grand Marnier, if using.

2. Cover with plastic wrap and refrigerate, stirring once or twice, until chilled, at least 2 hours. (The relish can be made up to 1 day ahead and refrigerated.)

Makes a scant 3 cups

VEGETABLES & SIDE DISHES

cranberry-
peach chutney

SERVE THIS "FRUIT SALAD" CHUTNEY JUST as you would the standard cranberry sauce: as an accompaniment to turkey, roast chicken, or hearty game dishes.

2 cups fresh or thawed frozen cranberries,
  picked over and rinsed

1 cup apple cider or juice

¾ cup packed light brown sugar

8 dried peach halves, cut into ½-inch dice

⅓ cup golden raisins

⅓ cup chopped crystallized ginger

⅓ cup (½-inch dice) red or orange bell pepper

⅓ cup finely chopped onion

¼ cup apple cider vinegar

1 ½-inch piece cinnamon stick

½ teaspoon salt

¼ teaspoon crushed red pepper flakes

Pinch of ground allspice

In a medium saucepan, bring all of the ingredients to a boil over medium-high heat. Reduce the heat to low and simmer, stirring occasionally, for 20 minutes, or until thickened. Remove from the heat, transfer to a bowl, and cool to room temperature. Store, covered and chilled, until ready to serve.

Makes 3 cups

Cranberry Creations

Cranberries have a versatility that extends far beyond the beloved turkey–cranberry sauce combination. The tart ruby beads make great gifts when cooked into jams and chutneys, then packaged in reusable containers tied with bows. Cranberries are sometimes hard to find out of season, so buy several bags while you can and freeze some for later in the year. Aside from the usual cranberry garland, you can decorate with these fruits by using them in door-size wreaths and smaller rings to fit around candlesticks. They can also be added to evergreen kissing balls and hung from entries. And they bring instant elegance to a bouquet of flowers: Add enough cranberries to fill a clear glass container one third high, then add long-stem roses and water as usual.

dill-glazed *cucumbers*

W ARM AS A CUCUMBER? THAT'S RIGHT. IF you've never had cooked cucumber before, you're sure to be a convert with this easy-to-make dish. Cucumbers are often overlooked as side dishes, being relegated to the salad bowl, but they have great versatility. The flavor of this dish borders on exotic, and by including fresh herbs, the cucumbers can be adapted to enhance any menu. Dill and parsley are good choices, as are chives, tarragon, and even mint. Use white pepper instead of black if you want to avoid having black specks on the cucumbers and herbs.

3 large cucumbers

2 tablespoons unsalted butter

½ teaspoon salt

Freshly ground pepper, to taste

1 ½ tablespoons minced fresh dill
  (optional)

1. Peel the cucumbers and slice lengthwise in half. With a teaspoon or a melon baller, scrape out the seeds and discard. Cut the cucumbers crosswise into ¼-inch-thick slices.

2. In a large skillet, melt the butter over medium-high heat. Add the cucumbers, season with salt and pepper, and cook, stirring occasionally, until the cucumbers are tender, 8 to 10 minutes. (The cucumbers can be made ahead to this point and set aside, covered, at room temperature, for up to 2 hours.

Reheat them over medium-low heat, stirring occasionally, being careful not to break the slices apart.)

3. Stir in the dill, if desired. Transfer the cucumbers to a serving dish and serve immediately.

Serves 8

brown butter green beans

b EANS AMANDINE SEEM SO 50'S, DON'T YOU think? We think it's high time we surprised our taste buds with fragrant brown butter and pecans, which give this dish a Southern twang. It would make a nice accompaniment to Peach Compote with Bourbon-Glazed Ham (page 60) and The Classic Hoppin' John (page 63).

2 pounds fresh green beans

3 tablespoons unsalted butter

½ cup pecans, coarsely chopped

Salt and freshly ground pepper, to taste

1. In a large pot of boiling salted water, cook the beans until just tender, 8 to 10 minutes. Drain thoroughly. (The beans can be prepared ahead to this point, covered, and refrigerated.)

2. In a large deep skillet, heat the butter over medium-high heat until golden brown and fragrant, 3 to 5 minutes. Stir in the pecans, then add the beans, tossing to coat. Season with salt and pepper and cook, stirring, until hot, 1 to 2 minutes. Transfer to a serving platter and serve immediately.

Serves 8

lemon-scented green beans

y OU'LL KNOW THAT A GREEN BEAN IS FRESH if it snaps when you break it. (Of course, the people at the supermarket might not appreciate your little experiment.) They need very little accompaniment, just a sprinkle of thyme (fresh is best) and dash of lemon zest (which adds a citrus taste without darkening the deep green color, the way lemon juice does).

2 pounds fresh green beans

2 tablespoons unsalted butter

1 teaspoon fresh thyme leaves or generous

¼ teaspoon dried

1 ½ teaspoons freshly grated lemon zest

Salt and freshly ground pepper, to taste

1. In a large pot of boiling salted water, cook the beans until just tender, 8 to 10 minutes. Drain thoroughly. (The beans can be prepared ahead to this point, covered, and refrigerated.)

2. In a large deep skillet, melt the butter over medium heat. Add the beans, sprinkle with the thyme and lemon zest, and season with salt and pepper. Cook, stirring frequently, until hot, 1 to 2 minutes. Transfer to a serving platter.

Serves 8

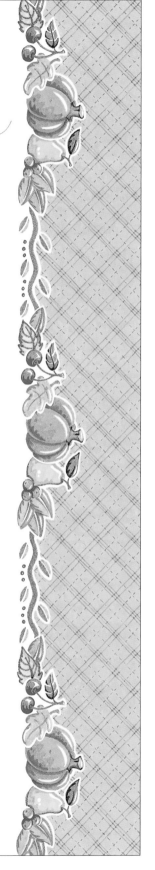

caramelized onions with
kale & bacon

1 IKE SERIOUS SKATERS AND SKIERS, KALE comes into its own in winter. A hearty plant, it can actually be left in the ground during the colder months, and the flavor improves after the frost, which is why the vegetable is so well timed for the holiday season. The caramelized onions and bacon give this dish sweet and smoky accents, making it the perfect foil for a holiday roast.

VEGETABLES &
SIDE DISHES

2 bunches kale, stems removed

2 cups water

4 slices bacon, cut crosswise into
   ¼-inch-thick slices

2 tablespoons olive oil

1 red onion, cut into ¼-inch-thick slices

2 garlic cloves, cut lengthwise into thin slices

¼ teaspoon salt

¼ teaspoon freshly ground pepper

1. To completely remove the stalks from the kale, even from the leafy portion, use one hand to hold each leaf rib side up, and use the other hand to strip the leaf off the stalk with one quick motion. Discard the stalks if tough; if tender, coarsely chop them. Cut or tear the leaves into bite-size pieces. Wash the kale thoroughly.

2. In a large deep skillet, bring the water to a boil over high heat. Add the kale and cook, covered, for 6 to 8 minutes, until softened. Drain in a colander. Wipe out the skillet.

3. In the same skillet, cook the bacon, stirring, over medium heat until crisp. Using a slotted spoon, transfer to paper towels to drain.

4. Pour off all but 1 tablespoon of the fat from the pan and add the oil. Heat over medium heat until hot but not smoking. Add the onion and garlic, and cook, stirring occasionally, for 10 minutes, or until lightly caramelized. Add the kale, salt, and pepper, and cook for 4 minutes, or until heated through. Transfer to a serving bowl and top with the crispy bacon.

Serves 8

fresh tarragon
creamed leeks

tHE HOLIDAYS ARE ALL ABOUT THE JOY OF familiar, once-a-year dishes, and also about adding something new to your family menu. This dish is sure to make you eager to experiment. A more sophisticated version of the popular creamed onions, creamed leeks have a delectable smoothness, an elegant French touch that is best appreciated in small servings. Make an effort to find fresh tarragon—it makes such a difference!—but if you can't, use fresh parsley instead.

4 bunches (4 to 5 pounds) leeks

2 tablespoons unsalted butter

**½ cup chicken stock, low-sodium canned
  chicken broth, or water**

¾ cup heavy cream

½ teaspoon salt, or to taste

⅛ teaspoon freshly ground pepper

**1 ½ tablespoons finely chopped fresh tarragon or
  flat-leaf parsley**

1. Trim off the root ends and dark green parts of the leeks. Cut each leek lengthwise in half, then cut crosswise into ¼-inch slices. In batches, put the leeks in a large colander and rinse well under cold running water to remove any grit; drain thoroughly.

2. In a large deep skillet, melt the butter over medium-high heat. Add the leeks and cook, stirring frequently, until translucent, about 10 minutes. Add the stock and bring to a simmer.

Reduce the heat, cover, and simmer very gently, stirring occasionally, until the leeks are very tender, 10 to 12 minutes.

3. Add the cream, salt, and pepper. Bring the mixture to a gentle simmer over medium-high heat, and cook until the cream is reduced and has thickened slightly, 5 to 8 minutes. Stir in the fresh tarragon or parsley. Transfer the leeks to a serving dish and serve immediately.

Serves 8

paprika-spiked
roasted mushrooms

iF YOU'RE FORTUNATE ENOUGH TO COME across wild mushrooms at the market, be sure to make this dish! It will make you seem like a creative cook, when all you really had to do was toss in the seasoning. Garlic and paprika give the mushrooms a Spanish flair and add complexity to their woodsy taste. Don't worry if you can't find the aforementioned wild or exotic mushrooms, though: Supermarket white button mushrooms also taste great when prepared this way.

2 pounds assorted mushrooms, such as shiitake (stemmed), cremini, oyster, chanterelle, and/or white, trimmed and cleaned

4 garlic cloves, minced

1 ½ teaspoons paprika

2 teaspoons salt

¼ teaspoon freshly ground pepper

¼ cup olive oil

3 tablespoons minced fresh parsley

1. Preheat the oven to 450°F.

2. In a large shallow roasting pan, toss the mushrooms with the garlic, paprika, salt, pepper, and oil, coating them evenly. Add the parsley and toss well. Spread the mushrooms out in the pan and roast, stirring once or twice, for about 20 minutes, or until tender and lightly browned. Transfer to a serving platter and serve immediately.

Serves 8

Timetable to a Fuss-Free Holiday

- Seven days before: Plan your menu. Note which dishes can be prepared ahead.
- Six days before: Check the recipes, the cupboards, and who's bringing what before making your grocery list.
- Five days before: If you're expecting a crowd, take inventory of chairs and tables. Clean out your refrigerator and freezer. Go shopping—preferably during off hours.
- Four days before: Start making side dishes that can hold for a few days, like chutneys. Get out napkins and tablecloths.
- Three days before: Continue making side dishes. Get out special serving ware.
- Two days before: Make your centerpiece and place cards. Start making extra ice and storing it in freezer bags.
- The day before: Chill wine.

lemon-buttered
parsnips

i F CARROTS COULD SOMEHOW BE CROSSED with nuts, parsnips would definitely be the result. The term "acquired taste" may apply to any number of winter root vegetables. As a group, they seem to share a somewhat pallid, gnarly appearance, so it's hard to visualize transformed into a sumptuous cooked side dish. But don't be discouraged: These sweet parsnips are heavenly, especially as prepared here, with an uplifting hint of lemon. The diagonal cut gives them an extra-special appearance.

3 pounds slender parsnips, peeled

⅓ cup minced fresh parsley

¼ cup (½ stick) unsalted butter

1 tablespoon chopped fresh thyme

¾ teaspoon finely grated lemon zest

½ teaspoon salt

⅛ teaspoon freshly ground pepper

1. Diagonally cut the parsnips into ½-inch slices.

2. In a steamer set over boiling salted water, steam the parsnips, covered, for about 8 minutes, or until tender when pierced with a fork.

3. Meanwhile, in a small saucepan, combine the parsley, butter, thyme, lemon zest, salt, and pepper and heat over medium heat until the butter has melted and the mixture is hot; reduce the heat and keep warm.

4. Transfer the parsnips and the butter mixture to a serving bowl. Toss to combine the ingredients and serve immediately.

Serves 8

spinach & parmesan
pearl onions

MORE OF A FESTIVE VEGETABLE CASSEROLE than a side dish, this variation on the classic Thanksgiving pearl onions in cream sauce gets style and substance from spinach and cheese. Because all of the vegetables are cooked individually before the final baking, they retain their distinctive flavors.

VEGETABLES &
SIDE DISHES

2 pounds pearl onions

3 tablespoons unsalted butter

1 garlic clove, minced

1 small bunch fresh spinach, tough stems removed
and well rinsed

¾ cup freshly grated Parmesan cheese

¼ cup heavy cream

¼ teaspoon salt

⅛ teaspoon freshly ground pepper

3 tablespoons unseasoned bread crumbs

1. Preheat the oven to 400°F.

2. In a large heavy saucepan, cover the onions with salted water and bring to a boil over high heat. Reduce the heat to low and simmer, uncovered, for 7 to 10 minutes, until the onions are tender when pierced with a fork. Drain and let cool. When cool enough to handle, slip the skins off the onions and trim the root ends.

3. In the same saucepan, melt 2 tablespoons of the butter over medium heat. Add the garlic and cook, stirring constantly, for 30 seconds, or until fragrant. Add the spinach and cook, stirring frequently, for 5 minutes, or until the spinach is wilted and the liquid has evaporated.

4. Stir in ½ cup of the cheese and the cream. Add the pearl onions, salt, and pepper and stir to combine. Transfer to a shallow 1-quart baking dish.

5. In a small bowl, combine the remaining ¼ cup cheese and bread crumbs. Sprinkle evenly over the onion mixture and dot with the remaining 1 tablespoon butter. Bake for 20 minutes, or until the top is lightly browned.

Serves 8

balsamic & thyme-glazed
pearl onions

WITH ITS HINTS OF CHESTNUT, MULBERRY, juniper and cherry, balsamic vinegar is just the right "mulled fruit" ingredient for a convivial holiday meal. It plays beautifully off the sweetness of the slightly caramelized onions and fresh thyme. Newly popular balsamic vinegar can range in price from a few dollars to a breathtaking $1,000 or more per bottle, but a modestly priced product will please all but the most sensitive, discriminating palate.

2 pounds pearl onions

¼ cup (½ stick) unsalted butter

1 tablespoon sugar

¼ teaspoon salt

⅛ teaspoon freshly ground pepper

2 tablespoons balsamic vinegar

2 teaspoons chopped fresh thyme leaves

1. In a large heavy saucepan, cover the onions with salted water and bring to a to a boil over high heat. Reduce the heat to low and simmer, uncovered, for 7 to 10 minutes, until the onions are tender when pierced with a fork. Drain and let cool. When cool enough to handle, slip the skins off the onions and trim the root ends.

2. In a large skillet, melt the butter over medium heat. Stir in the sugar, salt, and pepper and increase the heat to medium-high. Add the onions and cook, stirring occasionally, for 5 to 8 minutes, until the onions are glazed and golden brown. Stir in the vinegar and thyme and cook for 1 minute longer. Transfer the pearl onions to a bowl and serve immediately.

Serves 8

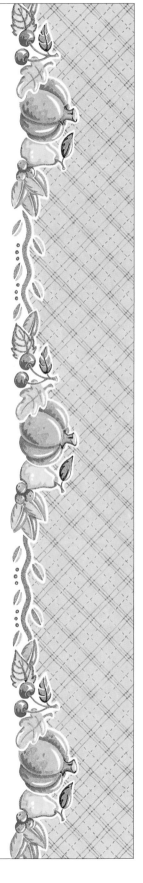

scallion & lettuce—
dressed peas

nOW, THERE'S ABSOLUTELY NO EXCUSE NOT to eat your peas! Glistening like tiny fairy ornaments, tiny tender peas have more flavor and sweetness than their more mature sisters. There really isn't an entree—beef, pork, fish, or poultry—that will not be that much better with a side bowl of peas with lettuce and scallions. If the great flavor isn't enough, this dish can be made without any advance preparation and is ready for the table in just minutes.

3 tablespoons unsalted butter

1 bunch (about 6) scallions, white and light
   green parts, thinly sliced

½ cup water

Three 10-ounce packages frozen petite peas

2 small heads Boston lettuce, quartered lengthwise
   and cut crosswise into thin slivers

1 teaspoon salt

¼ teaspoon freshly ground pepper

1 teaspoon fresh thyme leaves or generous
   ¼ teaspoon crumbled dried (optional)

1. In a large pot, melt the butter over medium-high heat. Add the scallions and cook, stirring occasionally, until translucent, about 3 minutes. Add the water and bring to a boil over high heat, then add the peas, lettuce, salt, pepper, and thyme, if desired, and bring back to a boil.

2. Reduce the heat to medium, cover, and cook, stirring occasionally, until the peas are tender and most of the liquid has evaporated, 3 to 5 minutes. Transfer the mixture to a serving bowl and serve immediately.

Serves 8

roasted

potato wedges

tHESE EASY POTATOES ARE DELICIOUS AS is, but even more so tossed with sage or grated Parmesan cheese. The roasted garlic cloves can be easily squeezed out of their skins and enjoyed along with the potatoes. Be sure to use Yukon Gold or a similar all-purpose variety rather than baking potatoes, which develop a mealy texture if cooked this way.

8 medium Yukon Gold or other all-purpose potatoes, cut lengthwise into quarters

1 large head garlic, separated into cloves but not peeled

2 ½ tablespoons olive oil

Salt and freshly ground pepper, to taste

1. Preheat the oven to 425°F. Generously oil a very large heavy baking sheet (or two smaller baking sheets).

2. In a large bowl, combine the potatoes and garlic, add the oil, and toss to coat. Season generously with salt and pepper. Spread out the potatoes, cut side down, and garlic in a single layer on the prepared baking sheet.

3. Bake for 18 to 20 minutes, turning the potatoes and garlic once or twice, until the potatoes are golden brown and tender. (If the potatoes stick when you try to turn them, let them stand at room temperature for 1 minute, then turn them and return them to the oven.) Serve the potatoes hot, with the softened garlic cloves.

◆ ## Roasted Potato Wedges with Sage

When the potatoes are done, transfer them to a large shallow bowl, add 2 tablespoons finely slivered fresh sage and 2 teaspoons olive oil, and toss well. Spread the potatoes and garlic out on the baking sheet again and bake for 1 to 2 minutes longer, until the sage is slightly wilted.

◆ ## Roasted Potato Wedges with Parmesan

When the potatoes are done, transfer them to a large shallow bowl, sprinkle with 6 tablespoons freshly grated Parmesan cheese, and toss to coat. Spread the potatoes and garlic out on the baking sheet and bake for 1 to 2 minutes longer, until the cheese begins to melt.

Serves 8

fresh chive-
potato gratin

WITH ITS SMOOTH BLEND OF MASHED POTA-toes and cheese, this soothing dish is comfort on a plate. Paired with a crispy salad, it could even serve as a main course on a holiday weeknight, after everyone returns from the Christmas pageant, too excited to eat a huge meal.

4. Preheat the broiler. Sprinkle the potatoes with the cheese and broil about 2 inches from the heat for 5 to 7 minutes, until the top is golden and crusty.

Serves 8

3 pounds baking potatoes, peeled and cut into ½-inch chunks

2 garlic cloves, peeled

½ cup heavy cream, at room temperature

¼ cup snipped fresh chives

2 tablespoons unsalted butter

½ teaspoon salt

¼ teaspoon freshly ground pepper

½ cup freshly grated Parmesan cheese

1. In a large saucepan, cover the potatoes and garlic with salted water and bring to a boil over high heat. Reduce the heat to low. Cover and simmer for 15 minutes, or until the potatoes are tender when pierced with a fork.

2. Drain the potatoes and garlic and return them to the pan. Heat over high heat, shaking the pan, for about 30 seconds, or until any liquid has evaporated.

3. Mash the potatoes and garlic until smooth and add the cream, chives, butter, salt, and pepper. Transfer the potato mixture to a 2-quart shallow broilerproof baking dish.

creamy scalloped

potatoes

IF YOU WANT TO BE FANCY AND INTERNA-
tional about it, call these potatoes a "gratin." But
by whatever name it's called, this dish is undeniably
first-class comfort food. Whether you're mounting a
fancy dinner or a casual supper, creamy scalloped potatoes are
a real crowd pleaser, especially when served with Rosemary-
Roasted Rack of Lamb (page 66). For thin-as-a-coin potato
slices, use a mandoline (vegetable slicer), available at kitchen-
ware stores.

the potatoes are golden brown on top and tender when
pierced with a small sharp knife. Let stand for 10 minutes
before serving.

Serves 8

2 ½ pounds baking potatoes

1 ¼ teaspoons salt

¼ teaspoon freshly ground pepper

1 ¾ cups heavy cream

1. Position a rack in the center of the oven and preheat the
oven to 325°F. Generously butter a 13- x 9-inch baking pan
and set aside.

2. Peel the potatoes. Using a mandoline or very sharp knife,
cut the potatoes into ⅛-inch-thick slices. Arrange one-quarter
of the potatoes in an even layer in the prepared dish and
sprinkle with a generous ¼ teaspoon of salt and a large pinch
of pepper. Gently pour a scant ½ cup of the cream over the
potatoes. Repeat the layering with the remaining potatoes,
salt, pepper, and cream.

3. Cover the pan with foil and bake for 30 minutes. Remove
the foil and bake uncovered for 20 to 30 minutes longer, until

french-style
mashed potatoes

SOUNDS MYSTERIOUS, DOESN'T IT? BUT THE Frenchness of this dish comes from its no-stint helpings of butter and cream. If you are serving this side dish for a Chanukkah celebration, substitute margarine for the butter and stock or broth for the cream. The results won't have the same creaminess as the original, but what a great dish to serve with Shiitake & Sage-Scented Pot Roast (page 51) or Peppered Beef Tenderloin (page 52).

can be prepared up to 1 hour ahead and set aside, partially covered, at room temperature. Reheat, stirring frequently, over medium-low heat.)

3. Transfer the potatoes to a serving bowl, sprinkle with the chives, if desired, and serve hot.

Serves 8

3 pounds Yukon Gold or baking potatoes,
    peeled and quartered lengthwise
1 cup heavy cream
6 tablespoons (¾ stick) unsalted butter,
    cut into pieces
¾ teaspoon salt, or to taste
¼ teaspoon freshly ground pepper
2 tablespoons finely chopped fresh chives,
    for garnish (optional)

1. In a large pot, cover the potatoes with salted water and bring to a boil over high heat. Reduce the heat to medium-high and boil for about 15 minutes, or until the potatoes are tender when pierced with a fork. Drain well.

2. Put the potatoes through a food mill or potato ricer, or mash with a potato masher in a large bowl, and return to the pot. Add the cream, butter, salt, and pepper and heat over low heat, stirring, until well blended and hot. (The potatoes

roasted-garlic
mashed potatoes

WHAT A STRING OF PEARLS DOES FOR A LITtle black cocktail dress, sweet roasted shallots and garlic do for homespun mashed potatoes. For the smoothest, creamiest texture possible, use Yukon Gold or Yellow Finnish potatoes.

> 12 shallots, unpeeled
>
> 1 head of garlic, outer skin peeled, leaving the head intact
>
> ¼ cup fruity olive oil, preferably extra-virgin
>
> Salt and freshly ground pepper, to taste
>
> 3 ½ pounds Yukon Gold, Yellow Finnish, or baking potatoes, peeled and cut into ½-inch chunks
>
> ¼ cup (½ stick) unsalted butter, at room temperature

1. Preheat the oven to 425°F.

2. On a large sheet of foil, toss together the shallots, garlic, and 1 tablespoon olive oil, and season with the salt and pepper. Tightly seal the foil and roast in the oven for 1 hour. Unwrap the package carefully—watch out for steam—and let cool. When cool enough to handle, peel the shallots and the garlic cloves. In a small food processor, process the shallots and garlic until pureed.

3. In a large saucepan, cover the potatoes with salted water and bring to a boil over high heat. Reduce the heat to low.

Cover and simmer for 15 minutes, or until the potatoes are tender when pierced with a fork. Drain, reserving about 1 cup of the cooking liquid.

4. Return the potatoes to the pot. Heat over high heat, shaking the pan, for about 30 seconds, or until any liquid has evaporated. Using a potato masher, mash the potatoes until they are smooth. Add the shallot-garlic puree, the remaining 3 tablespoons olive oil, and the butter and season with salt and pepper, adding enough of the reserved cooking liquid to reach the desired consistency. Transfer to a bowl and serve hot.

Serves 8

roasted red
onion relish

kEEP THIS CONDIMENT ON HAND TO GIVE A sweet kick to roast poultry, beef, lamb, or pork. Its color makes any dish instantly festive.

4 red onions, unpeeled

2 tablespoons olive oil

Salt

1 cup chicken or vegetable broth

1 tablespoon balsamic vinegar

1 tablespoon sugar

2 tablespoons finely chopped fresh cilantro

¼ teaspoon crushed red pepper flakes

1. Preheat the oven to 400°F. In a large cast-iron or other heavy skillet, toss the red onions with the olive oil and season to taste with salt.

2. Roast the onions in the oven, shaking the skillet occasionally, for 30 minutes, or until they are very soft to the touch. Remove from the oven and let the onions cool slightly. Cut in half through the root, and set aside to cool further.

3. Add the broth, vinegar, and sugar to the skillet. Bring the mixture to a boil over medium-high heat, scraping with a wooden spoon to loosen any browned bits in the bottom of the pan. Cook, stirring, for 10 minutes, or until the liquid is reduced to about 2 tablespoons.

4. Meanwhile, remove the papery outer skins from the onions when they are cool enough to handle, then cut them crosswise into thin slices. Add the onions to the skillet with the cilantro and red pepper flakes and stir to combine well. Season to taste with salt, transfer to a serving bowl, and serve at room temperature.

Makes 2 cups

For the Love of Onions

No tears allowed during the holidays! To keep crying to a minimum when cutting up onions, use a very sharp knife and cut the onions in one forward motion, which will keep you from crushing the onion and sending the juices (and vapors!) flowing. Other remedies: Cut the onion from the stem end first; cut with your mouth full of bread; or cut while occasionally dipping the knife in diluted lemon juice.

Store onions in a cool, dry place (not the refrigerator) for approximately 2 weeks.

asparagus
risotto

YES, YOU WILL HAVE TO STIR—AND STIR. But it will all be worth it for the results: a delectably creamy dish that sticks to the ribs on a snowy night. And like snowflakes, it has infinite variations: add cheese, shrimp, pesto sauce, sun-dried tomatoes, cooked zucchini and eggplant, fresh tomatoes . . . whatever appeals.

1 ½ pounds asparagus, trimmed, stalks sliced on
    the diagonal into ¾-inch pieces, tips left whole
    (keep the tips and stalks separate)

Four 14½-ounce cans low-sodium chicken broth

3 cups water, or more as needed

2 tablespoons olive oil

1 large onion, finely chopped

3 cups Arborio or other risotto rice

¾ cup dry white wine

¼ cup (½ stick) unsalted butter, cut into 4 pieces,
    at room temperature

3 tablespoons finely chopped fresh parsley (optional)

1 ½ tablespoons grated lemon zest

1 teaspoon salt, or more to taste

Freshly ground pepper, to taste

½ cup freshly grated Parmesan cheese,
    plus extra (optional), for serving

1. Bring a large pot of salted water to a boil. Add the sliced asparagus stalks and cook for 2 to 3 minutes, depending on their thickness. Add the asparagus tips and cook until the tips and stalks are just tender, about 2 minutes longer. Drain thoroughly and set the asparagus aside.

2. Meanwhile, combine the broth and 3 cups water in a large saucepan and bring just to a boil over high heat. Reduce the heat and keep the broth at a very gentle simmer.

3. In a large deep skillet, heat the oil over medium heat. Add the onion and cook, stirring occasionally, until translucent, 5 to 7 minutes. Add the rice and stir until it is coated with oil and beginning to turn opaque, 2 to 3 minutes.

4. Add the wine and cook, stirring constantly, until all of it has been absorbed by the rice. Add about ½ cup of the simmering broth and cook, stirring frequently, until it has been absorbed. Continue cooking, adding the broth ½ cup at a time and allowing it to be absorbed before adding more, until the rice is tender but still firm, about 20 minutes. The broth you add to the pan should bubble gently; adjust the heat as necessary. You may not need all of the broth, or you may need to add a little additional boiling water to the rice.

5. Gently stir in the asparagus, then stir in the butter, the parsley, if desired, the lemon zest, salt, and pepper. Cook, stirring, until the butter is melted and the asparagus is heated through. Stir in the Parmesan and serve immediately, with additional cheese on the side, if desired.

Serves 8

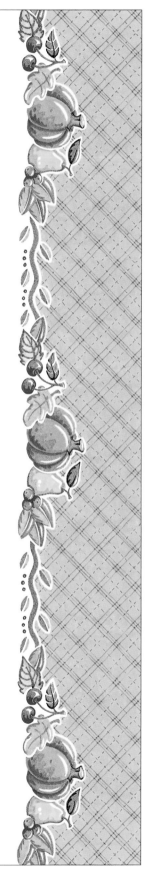

mushroom &

rye pilaf

a PRÈS SKI, SKATING, OR, YES, SHOPPING, warm up the family with this hearty Scandinavian-inspired dish. It's worth a special trip to the health-food store for the whole-grain rye.

Two .45-ounce packages dried mushrooms

6 cups hot water

¼ cup vegetable oil

2 red onions, finely chopped

2 garlic cloves, minced

Two 10-ounce packages small white mushrooms,
   stems discarded and caps thinly sliced

½ teaspoon salt

¼ teaspoon freshly ground pepper

2 cups whole-grain rye, rinsed and drained

1 cup golden raisins

¾ cup minced fresh parsley

1. In a medium bowl, soak the dried mushrooms in 1 cup of the hot water for 30 minutes. Reserving the liquid, rinse and finely chop the mushrooms. Strain the liquid through a strainer lined with a double thickness of damp paper towels set over a medium bowl; set aside.

2. Meanwhile, in a Dutch oven, heat the oil over medium heat. Add the onions and garlic and cook, stirring, for 4 minutes, or until softened. Add the sliced mushroom caps and cook, stirring, for 4 minutes, or until softened.

3. Add the remaining 5 cups hot water, the reserved mushroom liquid, the chopped mushrooms, salt, and pepper and bring to a boil. Stir in the rye and raisins and return to a boil. Reduce the heat to medium-low, cover, and simmer for 1½ hours, or until all of the liquid is absorbed.

4. Remove the pan from the heat, stir in the parsley, and let stand, covered, for 5 minutes. Transfer to a serving bowl.

Serves 8

maple-glazed
sweet potatoes

SO GRANDMA ALWAYS MADE HER SWEET potatoes with marshmallows? Now that you're no longer twelve, you'll love this grownup version—and, seriously now, so will the kids.

3½ pounds (6 to 8) sweet potatoes

5 tablespoons unsalted butter, at room temperature

½ cup pure maple syrup

1. Put the sweet potatoes in a large pot, add salted water to cover, and bring to a boil over high heat. Reduce the heat slightly and boil gently until the potatoes are just tender when pierced with a knife, 15 to 18 minutes. Drain and set aside to let cool slightly.

2. Preheat the oven to 375°F.

3. When the sweet potatoes are cool enough to handle, peel them, using your fingers or a paring knife. Cut the potatoes into ¼-inch-thick slices. Generously butter the bottom of a 13- x 9-inch baking dish with about 1 tablespoon of the butter. Layer half the potatoes in the dish and dot with half the remaining butter. Layer the remaining potatoes on top and dot with the remaining butter. (The potatoes can be prepared to this point several hours ahead, covered, and refrigerated. Bring to room temperature before proceeding.)

4. Drizzle the maple syrup evenly over the potatoes, cover the dish with aluminum foil, and bake for 30 minutes. Remove the foil and baste the potatoes with the cooking juices. Bake, uncovered, for 25 to 30 minutes longer, basting several times, until the potatoes are very tender and just starting to brown slightly on top. Serve the potatoes, spooning any juices remaining in the dish over the top of each serving.

Serves 8

mango chutney & mashed
sweet potatoes

WHEN YOU NEED A QUICK SIDE DISH THAT'S as pretty as it is flavorful, turn to this life saver. Since the chutney is ready-made, it saves time.

5. Using a potato masher, mash the sweet potatoes until they are smooth. Stir in the hot cream mixture and the chutney. Transfer to a serving bowl, garnish with the scallion greens, and serve immediately.

Serves 8

VEGETABLES &
SIDE DISHES

4 slender scallions

3 pounds sweet potatoes, peeled and cut into
　　2-inch chunks

1 cup heavy cream

2 tablespoons minced and peeled fresh ginger

½ teaspoon salt

¼ teaspoon freshly ground pepper

¾ cup Major Grey's mango chutney,
　　finely chopped

1. Thinly slice the scallions, keeping the white and green parts separate.

2. In a large saucepan, cover the sweet potatoes with salted water and bring to a boil over high heat. Reduce the heat to low. Cover and simmer for 20 minutes, or until the potatoes are tender when pierced with a fork.

3. Drain the potatoes and return them to the pan. Heat over high heat, shaking the pan, for about 30 seconds, or until any liquid has evaporated.

4. Meanwhile, in a small saucepan, heat the cream, scallion whites, ginger, salt, and pepper over medium heat until hot. Cover and keep warm.

oven-roasted
sweet potatoes

IF GUESTS ARE MILLING AROUND THE kitchen looking for something to do, here's a recipe that's easy to prepare and guaranteed to keep them contentedly busy. Hot from the oven, the sweet potatoes are crunchy on the outside and wonderfully sweet on the inside; in addition, the fragrant fresh rosemary and orange zest infuse the dish with an extra spark of sweetness.

⅓ **cup olive oil**

4 pounds sweet potatoes, peeled and cut into
   2- to 3-inch chunks

Grated zest of 1 orange

1 tablespoon chopped fresh rosemary

1 garlic clove, minced

½ **teaspoon salt**

¼ **teaspoon freshly ground pepper**

1. Preheat the oven to 450°F.

2. Pour the oil into a large roasting pan and heat the pan in the oven for 5 minutes. Remove the pan from the oven and add the sweet potatoes. Carefully stir to coat them evenly with the hot oil and return to the oven.

3. Roast the sweet potatoes, carefully shaking the pan and turning the potatoes every 10 minutes, for 50 to 60 minutes, until browned and crisp.

4. Meanwhile, in a small bowl, combine the orange zest, rosemary, garlic, salt, and pepper.

5. Drain the potatoes briefly on a paper towel–lined platter and transfer them to a serving bowl. Sprinkle with the orange zest mixture. Toss to coat, and serve immediately

Serves 8

butter-glazed
cherry tomatoes

WHEN FULL-SIZE TOMATOES LOOK AS WEARY as a Northeast winter, sprightly little cherry tomatoes are always cheerily red in the market. Newly introduced grape tomatoes, which as their name promises, are longer and less round, are also increasingly available in cold months. These little explosions of flavor, which take just minutes to prepare, are best cooked just before serving. Basil, tarragon, chives, and dill all work as well as parsley as an herbal accent.

VEGETABLES &
SIDE DISHES

◆ Note

For an even more festive look, use yellow cherry tomatoes or a mixture of yellow and red.

2 tablespoons unsalted butter

¼ cup minced shallots

2 pints small or medium cherry tomatoes

¼ teaspoon salt

Freshly ground pepper, to taste

2 tablespoons finely chopped fresh parsley
   (optional)

1. In a large skillet, melt the butter over medium-high heat. Add the shallots and cook, stirring, until they begin to soften, about 2 minutes.

2. Add the tomatoes, season with salt and pepper, and cook, stirring, until the tomatoes start to soften, 3 to 5 minutes. Stir in the parsley, if desired, and transfer to a serving dish.

Serves 8

bacon, pine nuts & *parsley wild rice*

tHERE'S A HOMEY QUALITY TO WILD RICE that makes it perfect at the traditional Thanksgiving dinner. The rice's nutty flavor has a natural affinity for pine nuts and bacon. Batches of rice can be prepared ahead of time and kept in the refrigerator for spur-of-the-moment gatherings. Covered tightly with plastic wrap, this rice dish will keep for three to four days. Leftover wild rice can be combined with any number of vegetable side dishes, and even added to homemade turkey soup.

4 slices bacon, cut crosswise into
    ¼-inch-thick slices

1 red onion, cut into ¼-inch dice

2 garlic cloves, minced

2½ cups water

2 cups chicken or vegetable broth

1½ cups wild rice, rinsed well and drained

1 small bay leaf

½ teaspoon salt

½ cup toasted pine nuts

3 tablespoons minced fresh parsley

¼ teaspoon freshly ground pepper

1. In a Dutch oven, cook the bacon, stirring, over medium heat until crisp. Using a slotted spoon, transfer to paper towels to drain. Set aside.

2. Pour off all but about 2 tablespoons of the fat from the pot and add the onion and garlic. Cook over medium heat, stirring, for 5 minutes, or until light golden brown. Add the water, broth, wild rice, bay leaf, and salt. Cover and bring the mixture to a boil over high heat. Uncover and simmer, without stirring, for 35 minutes, or until the rice is tender.

3. Drain the rice and return it to the pot. Heat over low heat, shaking the pan, for 5 minutes, or until any liquid has evaporated. Remove and discard the bay leaf. Stir in the reserved bacon, the pine nuts, parsley, and pepper and transfer to a serving bowl.

Serves 8

cheddar & chive biscuits

VEGETABLES &
SIDE DISHES

S OMETIMES IT SEEMS LIKE HOLIDAY MEALS are just an excuse to devour homemade biscuits. These light savory morsels should probably be made in a double batch to ensure that everyone gets his and her share. They're best straight from the oven, of course, but you could make them ahead of time and reheat. Spare not the butter!

2 cups all-purpose flour

1 tablespoon baking powder

¼ teaspoon baking soda

¾ teaspoon salt

6 tablespoons (¾ stick) cold unsalted butter, cut into ½-inch cubes

¾ cup grated (about 3 ounces) sharp Cheddar cheese

2 tablespoons minced chives or finely minced scallion greens

¾ cup plus 2 to 3 tablespoons buttermilk

1. Position a rack in the center of the oven and preheat the oven to 425°F.

2. In a large bowl, whisk together the flour, baking powder, baking soda, and salt. Using a pastry blender or two knives, cut in the butter until the mixture resembles coarse meal. With a fork, stir in the cheese and chives until well blended. Stir in ¾ cup plus 2 tablespoons of the buttermilk just until

combined; if the dough seems dry, stir in up to 1 more tablespoon buttermilk.

3. Turn the dough out onto a lightly floured surface and knead very briefly just until it comes together; do not overwork. With lightly floured hands, pat out the dough to a ½-inch thickness. Using a lightly floured 2-inch biscuit cutter (or a glass), cut out biscuits and place them about 1 inch apart on an ungreased baking sheet. Press the scraps of dough together, pat out again to a ½-inch thickness, and cut out more biscuits.

4. Bake for 14 to 16 minutes, until the biscuits have risen and are golden brown on top. Serve hot. (The biscuits can be baked up to 8 hours ahead. To reheat, wrap loosely in foil and reheat in a preheated 350°F oven for about 10 minutes.)

Makes about 1 dozen biscuits

pumpkin & cornmeal
spoonbread

CHILDREN WILL BE ENCHANTED BY THE IDEA of "spooning up" bread and eating it with a utensil. A Southern favorite, it lends itself to main courses of similar origin, such as Peach Compote with Bourbon-Glazed Ham (page 60).

1 ½ cups buttermilk

1 cup solid-pack canned pumpkin (not
 pumpkin pie mix)

4 large eggs, separated

3 tablespoons snipped fresh chives

1 ½ cups yellow cornmeal

1 tablespoon brown sugar

1 teaspoon baking soda

¾ teaspoon salt

⅛ teaspoon freshly ground pepper

1 ½ cups water

¼ cup (½ stick) unsalted butter

1. Preheat the oven to 350°F. Lightly oil a shallow 2½-quart ceramic baking dish.

2. In a large bowl, whisk together the buttermilk, pumpkin, the egg yolks, and 2 tablespoons of the chives. In a small bowl, whisk together the cornmeal, sugar, baking soda, salt, and pepper. Set aside.

3. In a large saucepan, bring the water and the butter to a boil over high heat. Remove the saucepan from the heat and gradually whisk the cornmeal mixture into the hot liquid until blended. Whisk in the pumpkin mixture.

4. In a medium bowl, beat the egg whites with an electric mixer at high speed just to stiff peaks. Gently fold the egg whites, one-third at a time, into the cornmeal mixture until well blended. Gently spoon the batter into the prepared baking dish and sprinkle with the remaining 1 tablespoon chives.

5. Place the baking dish in a roasting pan in the oven. Pour boiling water into the roasting pan until it reaches halfway up the side of the baking dish. Bake for 50 to 60 minutes, until lightly browned and puffed and a knife inserted 2 inches from the center comes out clean. Remove from the oven and serve immediately.

Serves 8

black pepper & cornmeal muffins

nOT TO BE MISTAKEN FOR BREAKFAST muffins, these savories get their bite from freshly ground pepper. Since your guests are surely going to want more, it's wise to bake up a few extra batches, wrap them tightly in plastic wrap and heavy-duty foil, and keep them in the freezer. They'll just need to be reheated before serving: Ten minutes at 350°F should do it!

1 ½ cups all-purpose flour

½ cup yellow cornmeal

2 teaspoons baking powder

1 teaspoon ground coriander

½ teaspoon salt

½ teaspoon freshly cracked pepper

1 ¼ cups milk

2 large eggs

2 tablespoons olive or vegetable oil

2 tablespoons unsalted butter,
   melted and cooled

1. Preheat the oven to 425°F. Lightly oil eight 2½-inch muffin cups. Set aside.

2. In a medium bowl, using a whisk, stir together the flour, cornmeal, baking powder, coriander, salt, and pepper. In another bowl, whisk together the milk, eggs, oil, and butter.

3. Pour the liquid mixture into the flour mixture and stir just until blended; do not overmix. Spoon the batter into the prepared muffin cups, filling each one about two thirds full.

4. Bake the muffins for 18 to 20 minutes, until the tops spring back when lightly touched. Immediately remove the muffins from the pan and cool slightly on wire racks.

Makes 8 muffins

Chapter Five

desserts & beverages

THE QUEEN OF THE KITCHEN

caramel syrup

over oranges

O RANGES SPARKLING IN CARAMEL MIGHT LOOK decadent, but don't feel guilty: Remember, you're eating fruit, not cake. As this is a make-ahead dessert, you can produce it at the last moment and then sit right down and enjoy it with your guests.

8 large seedless oranges

⅔ cup sugar

¼ cup water

6 tablespoons fresh orange juice

1 to 2 tablespoons Grand Marnier (optional)

8 mint sprigs, for garnish

1. Using a serrated or other sharp knife, cut a thin slice off the top and bottom of each orange to expose the flesh. Slice off the peel in strips, removing all the bitter white pith. Cut the oranges crosswise into ¼-inch-thick slices, removing any seeds, and put in a large shallow bowl.

2. In a large deep heavy saucepan, combine the sugar and water and bring to a boil over medium-high heat, stirring to dissolve the sugar. Brush down the sides of the pan with a wet pastry brush to remove any sugar crystals. Boil, without stirring, until the caramel is a deep golden amber color, 6 to 8 minutes.

3. Immediately remove the pan from the heat and, standing back to avoid splatters (the caramel will bubble up), add the orange juice. Stir with a wooden spoon until completely smooth; if necessary, return the pan to low heat and cook, stirring, until any hardened caramel has dissolved.

4. Remove the pan from the heat and let cool for about 10 minutes. Pour the caramel syrup over the oranges, tossing gently. (Don't worry if any hardened bits of caramel form—they will dissolve as the oranges sit.) Cover and refrigerate for at least 3 hours, stirring occasionally.

5. To serve, spoon the oranges and their syrup into shallow dessert bowls. Drizzle the Grand Marnier over the oranges, if desired, and garnish with the mint sprigs.

Serves 8

blue cheese & *caramelized pears*

t HE CHEESE COURSE IS A LOVELY IDEA, BUT usually a bit much after dessert. Instead, combine sweet and savory tastes in a single course. Start with the ripest pears you can find and roast them quickly at a high temperature to both caramelize them and heighten the flavor. Just a few bits of blue cheese make all the difference to this dish. Pears and blue cheese are a classic combination; the enzymes in the cheese react wonderfully with the pears.

8 ripe pears, such as Bosc

3 tablespoons unsalted butter, melted

8 teaspoons sugar

8 ounces good-quality blue cheese

1. Preheat the oven to 500°F. Line a large heavy baking sheet with foil.

2. Halve the pears lengthwise and core them (use a melon baller to remove the core from each half, then remove the tough fibers running from the stem end to the bottom of each half with a sharp paring knife). Place the pears, cut side up, on the baking sheet and brush with some of the butter, then turn cut side down and brush with the remaining butter.

3. Roast the pears for 10 to 15 minutes, or until the cut sides begin to color. Turn, cut side up, and carefully sprinkle ½ teaspoon of the sugar over each pear half. Roast for 5 to 10 minutes longer, or until tender when pierced with a knife. (The pears can be roasted up to 2 hours in advance and set aside, loosely covered, at room temperature. Reheat in a 350°F oven for 10 to 15 minutes before serving.)

4. Arrange 2 pear halves, cut side up, on each dessert plate. Crumble the blue cheese over the pears and serve immediately.

Serves 8

◆ Roasted Pears with Brie

Substitute 8 ounces Brie, cut into 8 small wedges, for the blue cheese. Place a wedge of Brie on each plate and arrange 2 pear halves next to it.

brown sugar
shortbread

tHIS SHORTBREAD COULDN'T BE EASIER: no chilling the dough or rolling it out—you just pat it into the pan and bake. And it's incredibly delicious, with a slight caramel flavor from the brown sugar and a delightfully crumbly texture. It makes a great Christmas or Chanukkah gift (if you can keep your family from eating it all up!) wrapped in a tin, attaching the recipe with a beautiful ribbon and ornament or dreidel.

4. Bake the shortbread for 50 to 55 minutes, or until it is golden brown (the edges will be slightly darker). Let cool on a wire rack for 5 to 10 minutes. With a sharp knife, cut the shortbread, still in the pan, into 36 rectangles. Let cool completely before removing from the pan.

Makes 3 dozen cookies

I cup (2 sticks) unsalted butter, at room
    temperature
⅓ cup packed light brown sugar
⅓ cup granulated sugar
I teaspoon vanilla extract
⅛ teaspoon salt
2 cups all-purpose flour

1. Preheat the oven to 325°F. Lightly grease a 13- x 9-inch baking pan.

2. In a large bowl, beat the butter and both sugars with an electric mixer at medium-high speed until light and fluffy. Beat in the vanilla, then beat in the salt. On low speed, gradually beat in the flour just until incorporated.

3. Turn the dough into the prepared baking pan and, with your fingertips and/or the back of a spoon, gently press it evenly over the bottom of the pan.

holiday butter
cookie cutouts

ONE OF CHANUKKAH'S SWEETEST PLEASURES is sharing homemade treats like these butter cookies, which lend themselves to shapes like dreidels and stars. Or design your own free-form creations from this easy-to-handle dough.

2 cups all-purpose flour

½ teaspoon baking powder

¼ teaspoon salt

10 tablespoons (1 ¼ sticks) unsalted butter,
at room temperature

¾ cup plus 2 tablespoons granulated sugar

1 large egg

1 ½ teaspoons vanilla extract

1 ½ cups confectioners' sugar, sifted

Assorted food colors

1. In a medium bowl, whisk together the flour, baking powder, and salt.

2. In a large bowl, beat the butter and granulated sugar with an electric mixer at medium-high speed until light and fluffy. Beat in the egg, then beat in the vanilla. On low speed, gradually add the flour mixture, stirring just until incorporated. Divide the dough into 4 pieces, shape each piece into a disk, wrap in plastic, and refrigerate for about 1 hour, or until firm enough to roll. (The dough can be made up to 2 days ahead.)

3. Preheat the oven to 350°F.

4. On a lightly floured surface, roll out the dough, one piece at a time, to a ⅛-inch thickness. Cut out shapes using assorted 2- to 2½-inch cookie cutters and place 1 inch apart on ungreased baking sheets. (The scraps of dough can be chilled and re-rolled once.) Bake the cookies for 8 to 10 minutes, until the edges are lightly browned. Cool for 1 to 2 minutes on the baking sheets, then transfer to wire racks to cool completely.

5. In a small bowl, combine the confectioners' sugar and just enough water to make a smooth icing that can be piped. Divide the dough between two or more bowls and tint with different food colors as desired. To decorate the cookies, scrape the icing into a pastry bag fitted with a very small plain tip and pipe outlines or borders, swirls and dots, or other designs onto the cookies. Let stand until the icing is set.

Makes about 6 dozen cookies

gingerbread cookies

Y OU'LL HAVE A HARD TIME DECIDING WHETHER to decorate with these beautiful cookies or just eat them. Oh, go ahead: Do a little of both.

COOKIES

3 cups all-purpose flour

I teaspoon baking powder

½ teaspoon baking soda

I tablespoon ground ginger

½ teaspoon ground cinnamon

¼ teaspoon ground cloves

¼ teaspoon ground nutmeg

³⁄₈ teaspoon salt

10 tablespoons (1 ¼ sticks) unsalted butter,
   at room temperature

¾ cup packed dark brown sugar

½ cup dark molasses

2 teaspoons vanilla extract

I large egg

ICING

3 cups confectioners' sugar, sifted

Assorted food colors

1. Make the cookies. In a medium bowl, whisk together the flour, baking powder, baking soda, ginger, cinnamon, cloves, nutmeg, and salt. Set aside.

2. In another large bowl, preferably the bowl of a heavy-duty electric mixer at medium speed, beat the butter and brown sugar until light and fluffy. Beat in the molasses, then beat in the vanilla. Beat in the egg. On low speed, gradually beat in the flour mixture. The dough will be stiff. Divide the dough into quarters, shape into disks, and wrap in plastic. Refrigerate for at least 3 hours, or overnight.

3. Preheat the oven to 350°F. Lightly grease two baking sheets.

4. On a lightly floured surface, roll out the dough, one piece at a time, to a ³⁄₈-inch thickness. Using assorted 2- to 2½-inch cookie cutters, cut out cookies and place 1 inch apart on the prepared baking sheets. (The scraps of dough can be chilled and rerolled once.)

5. Bake the cookies for 8 to 10 minutes, until puffed and very lightly browned around the edges. Cool for 1 to 2 minutes on the baking sheets, then transfer to wire racks to cool completely.

6. Make the icing. In a medium bowl, combine the confectioners' sugar and just enough water to make a smooth icing that can be piped. Divide the dough between two or more bowls and tint with different food colors as desired. To decorate the cookies, scrape the icing into a pastry bag fitted with a very small plain tip and pipe designs onto the cookies. Let stand until the icing is set.

*Makes about 6½ dozen
2 - to 2½ -inch cookies*

sugar-dusted sweet
apple fritters

CLOSE COUSINS TO APPLE LATKES, THESE sweet batter-dipped fried apple slices are a delicious treat to cook up on a cold winter afternoon—whether you're celebrating Chanukkah or just enjoying a cozy snow day.

1 ½ cups all-purpose flour

3 tablespoons granulated sugar

¼ teaspoon salt

3 large eggs, separated

1 cup milk

1 ½ tablespoons unsalted butter, melted

5 medium to large sweet-tart apples, such as
    Braeburn, Gala, or Granny Smith

2 tablespoons fresh lemon juice

Vegetable oil, for frying

Confectioners' sugar, for serving

1. In a large bowl, whisk together the flour, sugar, and salt.

2. In a medium bowl, whisk together the egg yolks and milk. Add to the flour mixture and stir just until smooth. Stir in the melted butter.

3. In a large bowl, beat the egg whites with an electric mixer at high speed just to stiff peaks. Using a large rubber spatula, gradually fold the whites into the milk mixture. Cover and set aside at room temperature.

4. Core the apples and cut them into ½-inch-thick slices; as you work, transfer the apples to a large bowl and toss them with the lemon juice.

5. Preheat the oven to 250°F. In a large heavy skillet, heat about ¼ inch oil over medium-high heat until very hot but not smoking. Add about 8 apple slices to the batter and stir gently with a fork to coat. One at a time, remove the apple slices from the batter, gently tapping off the excess, and add to the oil, without crowding. (The oil should be hot enough to sizzle vigorously as you add the apples.) Cook until golden brown on the first side, 3 to 4 minutes, then turn and cook until golden brown on the second side, about 3 minutes longer. Transfer to paper towels to drain briefly, then place on a baking sheet and keep warm in the oven while you fry the remaining apples. Add more oil to the pan as necessary, and allow the oil to reheat before adding more apples (if the oil is the proper temperature, you should not have to use much).

6. Serve the apples hot, sprinkled generously with confectioners' sugar.

Serves 8

green-apple
streusel tart

dURING THE HOLIDAY BUSTLE, YOU'LL appreciate this spicy dessert's time-saving step: You don't have to make a piecrust lid; just sprinkle on the crumbly brown sugar topping. Use cake flour for a texture soft as chiffon.

CRUST

1½ cups cake flour (not self-rising)

½ teaspoon baking powder

¼ teaspoon salt

½ cup (1 stick) cold unsalted butter, cut into pieces

2 to 3 tablespoons ice water

2 teaspoons fresh lemon juice

SPICY APPLE FILLING

6 large Granny Smith apples

½ cup packed light brown sugar

2 tablespoons all-purpose flour

1 teaspoon Chinese five-spice powder

¼ teaspoon salt

STREUSEL TOPPING

½ cup all-purpose flour

⅓ cup packed light brown sugar

¼ cup (½ stick) cold unsalted butter, cut into pieces

1. Make the crust. In the bowl of a food processor, combine the cake flour, baking powder, and salt and pulse just until blended. Distribute the butter evenly over the top of the flour mixture and pulse just until the mixture resembles coarse meal. Transfer to a medium bowl. In a small bowl, stir together 2 tablespoons of the ice water and the lemon juice. Drizzle the liquid over the flour mixture and with a fork stir just until moistened and the dough begins to hold together, adding the remaining 1 tablespoon of water only if necessary. The dough will be dry and crumbly, but should hold together when a small amount is pinched between your fingers. Gather the dough into a ball and shape it into a disk. Chill the dough for at least 30 minutes or overnight.

2. Preheat the oven to 425°F.

3. Between two sheets of waxed paper, roll out the pastry to a 12-inch round. Remove the waxed paper from one side, invert the pastry into a 10-inch tart pan with a removable bottom, and remove the second sheet of waxed paper. Chill the pastry until ready to fill.

4. Make the spicy apple filling. Peel, core, and slice the apples. In a large bowl, combine the sugar, flour, five-spice powder, and salt. Add the apples and toss to coat well. Transfer the mixture to the tart pan.

5. Make the streusel topping. In a small bowl, with a fork, stir together the flour, sugar, and butter until crumbly. Sprinkle the streusel evenly over the apples.

6. Bake the tart for 50 to 60 minutes, until the crust and the topping are dark golden brown and the apples are tender when pierced with a fork.

Serves 8 to 10

festive pear &  _pecan strudel_

O KAY—SO WE CHEATED ON THE USUAL ELAB-
orate strudel dough preparations. Just don't
tell your guests that you used ready-made phyllo
and no one will be the wiser. We can't think of a holiday
occasion where this wouldn't be a huge hit.

4 firm pears, peeled, cored, and cut into ½-dice

½ cup chopped pecans

¼ cup dried cranberries

Grated zest of 1 lemon

3 tablespoons light brown sugar

2 tablespoons brandy (optional)

10 sheets frozen phyllo dough, thawed

6 tablespoons (¾ stick) unsalted butter,
melted and cooled

3 tablespoons unseasoned bread crumbs

1. In a large bowl, combine the pears, pecans, cranberries,
lemon zest, sugar, and brandy, if desired.

2. Preheat the oven to 350°F. Butter a baking sheet and set
aside while preparing the strudel.

3. On a clean, dry work surface, lay out 1 sheet of the phyllo,
with the long side facing you. (Keep the remaining phyllo
sheets covered with a damp kitchen towel to prevent them
from drying out.) Brush the phyllo sheet with melted butter
and sprinkle lightly with bread crumbs; continue layering with
the remaining phyllo, butter, and bread crumbs.

4. Spoon the pear mixture along the long end of the phyllo,
about 2 inches from the edge. Roll up the strudel from the
long end, tucking in the shorter sides. Place the strudel, seam
side down, on the prepared baking sheet. Brush the top and
the sides of the strudel with any remaining melted butter.

5. Bake the strudel 35 to 40 minutes, until golden brown. Let
cool slightly before serving.

Serves 8

bittersweet
fudge pie

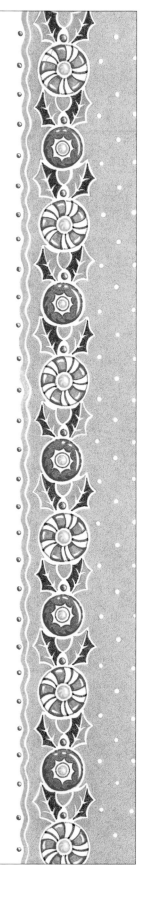

t HIS IS THE KIND OF DESSERT THAT SELLS out first at the church holiday bazaar. Flavorful but not too sweet, it satisfies even grownup obsessions for chocolate.

PIECRUST

1 ⅓ cups all-purpose flour

2 tablespoons sugar

¼ teaspoon salt

6 tablespoons (¾ stick) cold unsalted butter, cubed

2 tablespoons vegetable shortening, cut into pieces

2½ to 3½ tablespoons ice water

BITTERSWEET FUDGE FILLING

½ cup (1 stick) unsalted butter

4 ounces bittersweet or semisweet chocolate, coarsely chopped

4 large eggs

1¼ cups sugar

¼ teaspoon salt

1¼ teaspoons vanilla extract

Sweetened whipped cream, for serving

1. Make the piecrust. In the bowl of a food processor, combine the flour, sugar, and salt and pulse to blend. Scatter the butter and shortening over the flour and pulse about 10 times, until the mixture resembles coarse meal. Add 2½ tablespoons ice water and pulse just until the dough comes together, adding up to 1 tablespoon more water if necessary. Turn the dough out, shape into a disk, wrap in plastic, and refrigerate for at least 30 minutes, or overnight.

2. On a lightly floured surface, roll out the dough to a 12½-inch round. Fit it into a 9-inch glass pie plate and trim the edges, leaving a ½-inch overhang. Fold the excess dough under itself and flute the edge. Refrigerate for 30 minutes.

3. Position an oven rack in the lower third of the oven and preheat the oven to 375°F.

4. Line the pie shell with foil and fill with dried beans or rice. Bake for 15 minutes. Remove the foil and beans and bake for 8 to 10 minutes longer, until golden brown. Transfer to a wire rack to cool. Reduce the oven temperature to 350°F.

5. Make the bittersweet fudge filling. Combine the butter and chocolate in a small heavy saucepan and melt over low heat, stirring frequently until smooth. Remove from the heat.

6. In a large bowl, beat the eggs, sugar, salt, and vanilla with an electric mixer at medium speed until well blended. Beat in the chocolate-butter mixture. Pour the filling into the pie shell.

7. Bake the pie for 40 to 45 minutes, until the filling is puffed up and cracked around the edges and just set in the center. Transfer to a wire rack to cool completely. Refrigerate, loosely covered, for at least 3 hours, or until chilled. Cut the pie into wedges and top each serving with a dollop of whipped cream.

Serves 8

sour cream
pumpkin pie

eVERY THANKSGIVING MUST HAVE PUMPKIN pie—but there's no rule saying it must be the same old thing. This dessert gets its tang from sour cream in the filling, while a candied ginger garnish gives it a glistening sophistication. Or use leftover dough scraps to make decorative cutouts to add to the cooled baked pie at the last moment.

PIECRUST

1⅓ cups all-purpose flour

1½ tablespoons granulated sugar

¼ teaspoon salt

6 tablespoons (¾ stick) cold unsalted butter,
    cut into ½-inch cubes

2 tablespoons vegetable shortening,
    cut into 2 pieces

2½ to 3½ tablespoons ice water

SOUR CREAM–PUMPKIN FILLING

One 8-ounce container sour cream

2 large eggs

½ cup granulated sugar

⅓ cup packed light brown sugar

1 teaspoon ground cinnamon

1 teaspoon ground ginger

¼ teaspoon ground cloves

¼ teaspoon ground nutmeg

¼ teaspoon salt

One 16-ounce can solid-pack pumpkin (not pumpkin
    pie filling)

½ cup heavy cream

Finely slivered candied ginger, for garnish

Sweetened whipped cream, for serving

1. Make the piecrust. In the bowl of a food processor, combine the flour, granulated sugar, and salt and pulse to blend. Scatter the butter and shortening over the flour and pulse about 10 times, until the mixture resembles coarse meal. Add 2½ tablespoons ice water and pulse just until the dough comes together, adding up to 1 tablespoon more water if necessary. Turn the dough out, shape into a disk, wrap in plastic, and refrigerate for at least 30 minutes, or overnight.

2. On a lightly floured surface, roll out the dough to a 13-inch round. Fit it into a 9-inch glass pie plate and trim the edges,

leaving a ¾-inch overhang. Fold the excess dough under itself and flute the edge to form a high decorative rim. Refrigerate the dough for 30 minutes.

3. Position an oven rack in the lower third of the oven and preheat the oven to 375°F.

4. Line the pie shell with foil and fill with dried beans or rice. Bake for 15 minutes. Remove the foil and beans and bake for 8 to 10 minutes longer, until the pastry is golden brown. Transfer the pan to a wire rack to cool completely. Increase the oven temperature to 400°F.

5. Make the sour cream–pumpkin filling. In a small bowl, stir the sour cream briefly to loosen it. In a large bowl, beat the eggs until blended. With a wooden spoon, stir in both sugars, the cinnamon, ginger, cloves, nutmeg, and salt until combined. Stir in the pumpkin, sour cream, and cream just until blended. Pour the filling into the pie shell.

6. Bake for 45 to 50 minutes, until the filling is slightly puffed around the edges and a knife inserted in the center just comes out clean. (If the pastry starts to brown too much, cover the edges with strips of foil.) Transfer the pan to a wire rack to cool completely, at least 2 hours. Serve at room temperature, or refrigerate and serve chilled.

7. To serve, arrange a small mound of candied ginger in the center of the pie. Cut the pie into wedges and serve with whipped cream.

Serves 8

hard sauce–topped
mincemeat tartlets

WHAT IS MINCEMEAT? A LUSCIOUS COMBI-nation of fruits and spices. Made by Grandma's traditional methods, it's a time-consuming dish, but nowadays you can buy it at the store, saving yourself a few hours. If you like, make the hard sauce two days in advance and chill until the day you're using it; bring to room temperature before serving.

EGG PASTRY

2 large hard-cooked egg yolks

2 cups all-purpose flour

¼ cup granulated sugar

2 teaspoons grated lemon zest

¼ teaspoon salt

¾ cup (1 ½ sticks) cold unsalted butter, cut into pieces

2 large egg yolks, lightly beaten

2 tablespoons ice water

PEAR-MINCEMEAT FILLING

4 cups store-bought mincemeat

2 firm pears, peeled, cored, and finely chopped

HARD SAUCE

½ cup (1 stick) unsalted butter, at room temperature

2 cups sifted confectioners' sugar

2 tablespoons brandy

1 tablespoon grated lemon zest

Pinch of salt

1. Make the egg pastry. Using a rubber spatula, press the hard-cooked egg yolks through a sieve into a small bowl. In a medium bowl, with a fork, stir together the flour, hard-cooked egg yolks, granulated sugar, lemon zest, and salt until well combined. Add the butter, and with a pastry blender or two knives, cut it in until the mixture resembles coarse meal. In a small bowl, with a fork, stir together the egg yolks and water. Drizzle the mixture over the flour and, with a fork, stir just until combined. Shape the dough into a large disk and refrigerate, tightly wrapped in plastic, for at least 1 hour, or up to 2 days.

2. Make the pear-mincemeat filling. In a large bowl, stir together the mincemeat and pears. Set the mixture aside.

3. Place a rack in the middle of the oven and preheat the oven to 375°F.

4. Remove the dough from the refrigerator and cut the disk into 8 wedges. Lightly flour a sheet of waxed paper. Shape a wedge of dough into a small disk, sprinkle with a little flour, and top with another sheet of waxed paper. Roll the dough out to a round a little more than ⅛ inch thick. Peel off the top piece of waxed paper and invert the dough into a 4-inch tart-let pan. Peel off and discard the second piece of waxed paper. Gently press the dough against the bottom and sides of the pan, patching if necessary, and trim the excess even with the edges of the pan. Gather the scraps into a ball and reserve. Repeat with the remaining dough.

5. Fill the tartlet pans with the mincemeat filling.

6. To make the lattice top for the tartlets, roll out the reserved pastry between two sheets of waxed paper to make a rectangle about ¼ inch thick. Using a pastry wheel or knife, cut the dough into ¼-inch-wide strips slightly longer than the diameter of the tartlet pans. Lay 3 of the lattice strips evenly across each tartlet. Lay 3 more strips across these, either at right angles or on the diagonal. Trim the edges of the strips even with the edge of the tartlets.

7. Place the tartlets on a large baking sheet. Bake for 40 to 45 minutes, until the pastry is golden brown. Transfer the tartlets to wire racks and let cool completely.

8. Make the hard sauce. In a medium bowl, beat the butter with an electric mixer at medium speed until smooth. Gradually add the confectioners' sugar and beat until smooth. Add the brandy, zest, and salt and beat until fluffy. Top the tartlets with the sauce and serve.

Serves 8

cranberry pie with *hazelnut crust*

W E'VE POPPED CRANBERRIES OUT OF THE side dish category and restyled them as a sleek, sparkling dessert. It makes a tasty breakfast, too, with a mug of fragrant coffee or tea on Christmas morning.

FLAKY HAZELNUT CRUST

½ cup hazelnuts

1 ¾ cups all-purpose flour

½ cup confectioners' sugar

½ teaspoon grated lemon zest

½ teaspoon ground cinnamon

½ cup (1 stick) cold unsalted butter, cut into pieces

1 large egg, lightly beaten

CRANBERRY FILLING

One 12-ounce bag fresh or thawed frozen cranberries

1 cup granulated sugar

¼ cup water

1. Preheat the oven to 375°F.

2. Make the flaky hazelnut pastry. On a jelly-roll pan, roast the hazelnuts for 8 to 10 minutes, until fragrant and golden brown. In a kitchen towel, rub the nuts together to remove the skins; discard the skins. Let the nuts cool completely.

3. In a food processor, pulse the nuts just until finely ground. Add the flour, confectioners' sugar, zest, and cinnamon and process for about 10 seconds, just to combine. Distribute the butter on top of the flour and pulse until the mixture resembles coarse meal. Measure 1½ tablespoons of the egg and refrigerate, for glazing the pie. Drizzle the remaining egg over the crust ingredients and process just until the dough begins to come together. Shape the dough into a disk, wrap in plastic, and refrigerate for at least 30 minutes, or overnight.

4. Meanwhile, make the cranberry filling. In a medium saucepan, bring the cranberries, granulated sugar, and water to a boil. Boil, stirring constantly, over high heat about 5 minutes, until very thick and jamlike. Let the filling cool completely.

5. Preheat the oven to 375°F.

6. Roll out two-thirds of the dough to a 12-inch round and trim the edge. Press the pastry into the bottom and up the sides of a 9-inch springform pan. Roll the remaining pastry into a 9- to 10-inch circle and cut into eleven ½-inch-wide strips. On a baking sheet, freeze the strips for 3 to 5 minutes to firm.

7. Spoon the cooled filling into the pie shell and, with a rubber spatula, smooth the top.

8. Lift the pastry strips off the baking sheet with a table knife. Arrange eight of the strips 1½ inches apart in a lattice pattern on top of the filling. Fold the ends into the filling.

9. To make a decorative crimped edge, press the remaining 3 strips around the top edge of the pastry to make a continuous smooth circle, trimming as needed. Insert a thin metal spatula between the pastry and the side of the pan and push

the pastry slightly away from the pan; continue all around the edge. Place the end of a thin wooden spoon or chopstick on the inside edge, and, with the spoon, push the pastry against your fingers to crimp it. Repeat all around the edge. Brush the lattice with the reserved egg.

10. Bake for 40 to 45 minutes, until the pastry is golden brown. Cool the pie on a wire rack for 20 minutes. Remove the side of the pan and let the pie cool completely before serving.

Serves 10

pumpkin cheesecake with
gingersnap crust

WOULD YOU RATHER HAVE PUMPKIN PIE OR a luscious cheesecake for your holiday dessert? Make this and you and your guests won't have to make that terribly difficult choice.

DESSERTS & BEVERAGES

GINGERSNAP CRUST

1 ½ cups crushed gingersnap cookies

½ cup chopped pecans

6 tablespoons (¾ stick) unsalted butter, melted

¼ cup granulated sugar

PUMPKIN-CREAM CHEESE FILLING

1 ½ pounds cream cheese, at room temperature

½ cup packed light brown sugar

¼ cup granulated sugar

2 large eggs

2 large egg yolks

1 ½ tablespoons all-purpose flour

1 teaspoon ground cinnamon

½ teaspoon ground cloves

½ teaspoon ground ginger

½ teaspoon ground nutmeg

1 cup solid-pack pumpkin puree (not pumpkin pie mix)

½ cup sour cream

2 teaspoons pure vanilla extract

Pecan halves, for garnish (optional)

1. Preheat the oven to 350°F. Lightly butter an 8-inch spring-form pan.

2. Prepare the gingersnap crust. In a medium bowl, with a fork, combine all of the ingredients until the crumbs are evenly moistened. Press the mixture evenly over the bottom and up the side of the prepared pan. Bake the crust for 10 minutes and transfer to a wire rack to cool completely. Increase the oven temperature to 425°F.

3. Prepare the pumpkin–cream cheese filling. In a medium bowl, beat the cream cheese, brown sugar, and granulated sugar with an electric mixer at medium speed until light and fluffy. Beat in the eggs and the egg yolks, one at a time. Reduce the speed to low and add the flour, cinnamon, cloves, ginger, and nutmeg and beat until well blended. Add the pumpkin puree, sour cream, and vanilla and beat just until blended. Pour the filling into the pie shell.

4. Bake the cheesecake for 15 minutes. Reduce the heat to 250°F and continue baking for 1 hour. Turn the oven off and let the cheesecake cool in the oven for 3 hours. If desired, refrigerate the cake before serving.

5. To serve, run a knife around the side of the cheesecake to loosen. Remove the side of the pan and garnish the top with the pecan halves, if desired.

Serves 10

chocolate chestnut
cheesecake

fROM THE AMBROSIAL FILLING TO THE vanilla-spiked whipped cream topping, this cheesecake is rich every step of the way. Naturally, it must be doled out in small slices.

CRUST

2 cups sifted all-purpose flour

⅔ cup sugar

¼ teaspoon salt

1 cup (2 sticks) unsalted butter, at room temperature

CHOCOLATE-CHESTNUT FILLING

6 ounces semisweet chocolate

2 ounces unsweetened chocolate

3 cups ricotta cheese

One 15½-ounce can sweetened chestnut puree

6 large eggs, lightly beaten

1 cup sugar

2 teaspoons vanilla extract

1 cup sour cream

Vanilla whipped cream, for garnish

Candied whole chestnuts, for garnish (optional)

1. Make the crust. Into a medium bowl, sift together the flour, sugar, and salt. With a pastry blender or two knives, cut in the butter until the mixture resembles coarse meal. Form the dough into a ball, then press evenly over the bottom and up the side of a 10-inch springform pan. Refrigerate for at least 1 hour or overnight.

2. Preheat the oven to 350°F.

3. Make the chocolate-chestnut filling. In a small saucepan, melt both the chocolates, stirring until smooth, over low heat. Remove the pan from the heat and let cool.

4. In a large bowl, beat the ricotta with an electric mixer at high speed until smooth. Reduce the speed to low and add the chestnut puree and beat until well combined. Increase the speed to high and beat, scraping down the sides of the bowl occasionally, for 5 minutes, or until very smooth. Beat in the eggs, one at a time. Add the sugar, melted chocolate, vanilla, and sour cream and beat until smooth. Pour into the pie shell and smooth the top.

5. Bake the cheesecake for 1½ hours, or until the center is firm. Cool the cheesecake in the pan on a wire rack for 1 hour. Refrigerate, covered, for at least 4 hours or overnight.

6. Let the cake stand at room temperature for 30 minutes before serving. Remove the side of the springform pan. With a spatula, spread the whipped cream over the top of the cake or fill a pastry bag fitted with a star tip and pipe the cream along the edge. Garnish with candied whole chestnuts, if desired.

Serves 10 to 12

snowy black *forest cake*

hOLIDAY ENTERTAINING IS ALL ABOUT GOING the extra mile—or at least giving the impression that you did. This four-layer cake is much easier to put together than it looks. And to make things simpler still, you can bake and freeze the layers up to a month in advance. The cherries gleaming on the frothy whipped cream are as festive as holly berries in snow.

CHOCOLATE CAKE LAYERS
1 ½ cups plus 2 tablespoons all-purpose flour
½ cup Dutch-process cocoa powder
1 ½ teaspoons baking powder
½ teaspoon baking soda
½ teaspoon salt
10 tablespoons (1 ¼ sticks) unsalted butter,
   at room temperature
1 ¼ cups sugar
3 large eggs, at room temperature
1 ½ teaspoons vanilla extract
One 8-ounce container sour cream

CHERRIES AND SOAKING SYRUP
Two 16-ounce cans dark sweet cherries in syrup
1 tablespoon sugar
2 tablespoons kirsch (cherry-flavored liqueur)

FILLING AND FROSTING
3 cups heavy cream
¼ cup plus 1 tablespoon sugar
1 ½ to 2 tablespoons kirsch

GARNISH
12 candied cherries (optional)
Chocolate shavings

1. Make the cake layers. Preheat the oven to 350°F. Grease and flour two 9-inch round cake pans.

2. In a medium bowl, whisk together the flour, cocoa, baking powder, baking soda, and salt.

3. In a large bowl, beat the butter and sugar with an electric mixer at medium speed until light and fluffy. Add the eggs, one at a time, beating well after each addition. Beat in the vanilla. On low speed, beat in half the flour mixture. Beat in the sour cream, then beat in the remaining flour mixture. Pour the batter into the prepared pans and smooth the tops.

4. Bake for 25 to 30 minutes, or until a toothpick inserted in the center comes out clean. Let the layers cool in the pans on a wire rack for 10 minutes. Invert each layer onto a wire rack, then turn right side up onto another rack and let cool completely. (When completely cooled, the layers can be wrapped in plastic and stored at room temperature for up to 2 days or frozen for up to 1 month.)

5. Make the soaking syrup. Drain the cherries, reserving ¼ cup of the syrup. Spread them on a paper towel–lined plate and set aside. Combine the reserved syrup and the sugar in a small saucepan and bring to a boil over medium heat, stirring to dissolve the sugar; boil for 1 minute. Transfer to a small bowl and let cool slightly, then stir in the kirsch.

6. Make the filling and frosting. In a large bowl, beat the cream with the sugar and kirsch until stiff peaks form.

7. Using a long serrated knife, slice each cake layer horizontally in half. Place the bottom half of 1 cake layer on a serving plate and brush generously with the soaking syrup. Spread about 1 cup whipped cream evenly over the top and arrange one-third of the cherries on top, making sure to place some cherries around the edge of the cake to support the next layer. Place the top of the first layer on top, brush with syrup, and top with another 1 cup cream and half of the remaining cherries. Place the bottom half of the second cake layer on top, brush with syrup, and top with another 1 cup cream and the remaining cherries. Brush the top of the remaining layer with syrup and place on top of the cake. Reserve a generous ½ cup of the whipped cream for garnish. Frost the top and sides of the cake with the remaining whipped cream. Place the reserved whipped cream in a pastry bag fitted with a small star tip and pipe 12 rosettes around the top edge of the cake. Place a candied cherry, if using, on each rosette. Scatter chocolate shavings over the top of the cake. Refrigerate until ready to serve.

Serves 12

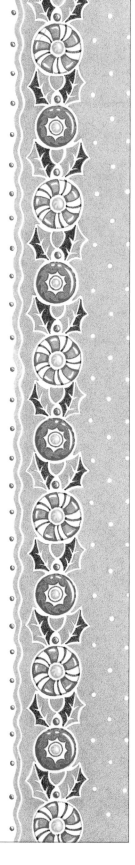

lemon cocoa
holiday panforte

WE LIKE TO IMAGINE THIS 16TH-CENTURY sweet from Siena being served in a Tuscan abbey by candlelight. The tastes of the local Italian countryside—almonds and figs—give the dessert its sweetness and crunch, perfect with a cup of espresso. It won't rise, so don't expect the dessert to be regulation cake height.

DESSERTS &
BEVERAGES

1 ½ cups toasted slivered almonds

1 ½ cups chopped stemmed dried figs

½ cup ¼-inch diced candied lemon peel

½ cup ¼-inch diced crystallized ginger

¾ cup all-purpose flour

½ cup unsweetened cocoa

1 teaspoon ground coriander

1 teaspoon grated lemon zest

½ teaspoon ground cinnamon

⅔ cup sugar

⅔ cup honey

Confectioners' sugar, for serving

1. Preheat the oven to 300°F. Butter a 9-inch springform pan, line the bottom with parchment paper, and butter the paper.

2. In a large bowl, stir together the almonds, figs, lemon peel, ginger, flour, cocoa, coriander, lemon zest, and cinnamon; mix well.

3. In a small saucepan, combine the sugar and the honey and cook, stirring with a wooden spoon, over medium heat until the sugar dissolves. Bring the mixture to a boil over medium-high heat and boil, stirring occasionally, until the mixture forms a firm ball when dropped into cold water, or it reaches 245°F on a candy thermometer. Immediately pour the mixture over the dry ingredients and, with a wooden spoon, stir quickly until there are no dry spots. Transfer the mixture to the prepared pan and with a wet rubber spatula, spread the batter evenly.

4. Bake for 50 minutes. The cake will still look soft but will firm as it cools. Cool the panforte completely on a wire rack. Remove the side of the pan and invert the panforte onto a piece of waxed paper. Carefully peel off the parchment paper. (The panforte may be stored, wrapped in foil, at room temperature for up to 1 week.)

5. Before serving, sprinkle with confectioners' sugar. Serve cut into very thin slices.

Serves 12 to 16

graham cracker
coffee cake

iN EUROPE, THERE IS A LOVELY TRADITION of celebrating the holiday morning with an elaborate coffee cake. At Easter, the dough is braided around colored eggs before it is baked; Christmas coffee cakes often include candied fruits, and, in Scandinavia, the St. Lucia's ring wears a fabulous crown of lighted candles. This coffee cake is a version of the American crumb cake: Graham crackers, cake, and a sweet glaze come together to bring you a Christmas morning treat. If you'd like to serve it more than once during the holiday week, try out the variations. Gingersnaps have a more intense flavor than graham crackers, and lemon streusel is pure holiday heaven.

CRUMBS

⅓ cup all-purpose flour

¼ cup packed light brown sugar

½ teaspoon pumpkin pie spice

¼ cup (½ stick) unsalted butter, at room temperature

⅓ cup graham cracker crumbs

CAKE

1¼ cups all-purpose flour

¾ teaspoon baking powder

½ teaspoon pumpkin pie spice

½ teaspoon baking soda

½ teaspoon salt

½ cup (1 stick) unsalted butter, at room temperature

1 cup packed light brown sugar

2 large eggs

⅓ cup buttermilk

CONFECTIONERS' SUGAR GLAZE

½ cup confectioners' sugar

1 tablespoon fresh lemon juice

1. Preheat the oven to 350°F. Butter a 9-inch-square baking pan.

2. Make the crumbs. In a medium bowl, combine the flour, brown sugar, and pumpkin pie spice with a fork, breaking up any large lumps of sugar with your fingers. Cut the butter in with a pastry blender or 2 knives until the mixture resembles coarse meal. Stir in the graham cracker crumbs and mix thoroughly. Set aside.

3. Make the cake. Sift the flour, baking powder, pumpkin pie spice, baking soda, and salt onto a sheet of waxed paper.

4. In a large bowl, beat the butter with an electric mixer at high speed until light and fluffy. Gradually beat in the brown sugar and continue to beat until well combined. Reduce the speed to medium and beat in the eggs one at a time, beating well after each addition. Reduce the speed to low and alternately beat in the flour mixture and the buttermilk, beginning and ending with the flour mixture; beat just until blended. Transfer the batter to the prepared pan and smooth the top with a rubber spatula. Sprinkle the crumbs evenly over the top, lightly pressing them into the batter.

5. Bake the cake for 35 to 40 minutes, until a cake tester inserted into the center comes out clean. Cool the cake in the pan on a wire rack.

6. Make the confectioners' sugar glaze. In a small bowl, stir together the confectioners' sugar and lemon juice with a fork until smooth.

7. Before serving, drizzle with the confectioners' sugar glaze over the coffee cake and let stand for 10 minutes, or until the glaze is set. Transfer the cake to a serving plate.

Serves 8

◆ Gingersnap Coffee Cake

Follow the recipe instructions for Graham Cracker Coffee Cake with these changes:

Crumbs: Substitute dark brown sugar for the light brown sugar, 1 teaspoon ground ginger and ½ teaspoon ground cinnamon for the pumpkin pie spice, and gingersnap crumbs for the graham cracker crumbs.

Cake: Substitute dark brown sugar for the light brown sugar, 1 teaspoon ground ginger and ½ teaspoon ground cinnamon for the pumpkin pie spice, and sour cream for the buttermilk.

◆ Lemon-Streusel Coffee Cake

Follow the recipe instructions for the Graham Cracker Coffee Cake with these changes:

Crumbs: Omit the pumpkin pie spice and substitute ⅓ cup sliced natural almonds for the graham cracker crumbs.

Cake: Add 1 tablespoon grated lemon zest to the batter with the eggs and substitute lemon-flavored yogurt for the buttermilk.

chocolate raspberry
truffle torte

tO CROWN A GLAMOROUS MIDNIGHT SUPPER, you won't do better than this torte. Fragrant with raspberry liqueur, it can be made ahead and capped off with the whipped cream topping shortly before serving. Or serve the whipped cream on the side, so that leftovers don't get soggy. If you'd rather forego the whipped cream, just dust this dense flourless creation with confectioners' sugar, using a snowflake template.

CHOCOLATE TORTE

12 ounces bittersweet chocolate, coarsely chopped

1 ½ cups sugar

Pinch of salt

¾ cup boiling water

1 ½ cups (3 sticks) unsalted butter, cut into pieces,
   at room temperature

6 large eggs, at room temperature

1 tablespoon Chambord or other raspberry-flavored
   liqueur or 2 teaspoons vanilla extract

WHIPPED CREAM TOPPING

1 ½ cups heavy cream

1 ½ tablespoons sugar

2 teaspoons Chambord or 1 ½ teaspoons
   vanilla extract

Grated chocolate, for garnish

Raspberries, for garnish (optional)

1. Make the chocolate torte. Preheat the oven to 350°F. Lightly butter the bottom of a 9-inch springform pan. Line the bottom of the pan with a round of waxed paper and butter the paper and the sides of the pan.

2. Combine the chocolate, sugar, and salt in the bowl of a food processor and process until the chocolate is finely ground. With the processor running, add the boiling water through the feed tube and process for about 15 seconds, until the chocolate is completely melted. Scrape down the sides of the processor bowl, then add the butter and process for about 5 seconds, until the batter is smooth. Add the eggs and Chambord and process until smooth. Pour the batter into the prepared pan.

3. Bake for 50 to 55 minutes, or until the edges of the torte are puffy and cracked and the center is just set (it will still look moist). Transfer the pan to a wire rack to cool for 30 minutes (the torte will sink as it cools). Cover the pan and refrigerate for 3 hours.

4. Remove the sides of the springform pan and invert the torte onto a flat serving platter. Gently press down on the cake if necessary to level it, then lift off the bottom of the springform pan and peel off the waxed paper. Cover and refrigerate until ready to garnish the torte. (The torte can be refrigerated for up to 2 days.)

5. Shortly before serving, make the whipped cream topping. In a large bowl, combine the cream, sugar, and Chambord and

beat until stiff peaks form. Spread the whipped cream over the top of the torte and use the back of a large spoon to create swirls and peaks of cream. (You can also cover the top of the torte with a very thin layer of the cream, then pipe on the remaining cream, using a pastry bag fitted with a medium star tip to create swirls or rosettes.) Sprinkle the grated chocolate over the cream and garnish with the raspberries, if desired.

Serves 8 to 10

dark chocolate
bûche de noël

tHIS IS THE CLASSIC DESSERT THAT CROWNS the French Christmas Eve feast. If you stroll through Paris around the holidays, every pastry shop window will be filled with these tasty "Yule logs."

DESSERTS & BEVERAGES

SPONGE CAKE

¼ cup (½ stick) unsalted butter, melted

5 large eggs, at room temperature

1 cup granulated sugar

1 teaspoon vanilla extract

1 cup cake flour (not self-rising), sifted

Confectioners' sugar, for dusting

CHOCOLATE FROSTING

12 ounces bittersweet or semisweet chocolate, coarsely chopped

1 ¾ cups heavy cream

2 tablespoons unsalted butter, cut into 4 pieces

1 ½ teaspoons vanilla extract

WHIPPED CREAM FILLING

4 ounces bittersweet or semisweet chocolate, coarsely chopped

2 tablespoons unsalted butter, cut into 4 pieces

1 cup plus 2 tablespoons heavy cream

2 tablespoons granulated sugar

¾ teaspoon vanilla extract

1. Make the sponge cake. Preheat the oven to 350°F. Lightly butter the bottom of a 15- x 10-inch baking sheet and line with waxed paper. Butter and flour the paper and the sides of the pan.

2. Pour the melted butter into a small bowl. In a large bowl, preferably the bowl of a standing electric mixer, combine the eggs, granulated sugar, and vanilla and beat at low speed until well blended. Increase the speed to high and beat until the mixture is pale, thick, and almost tripled in volume, 5 to 7 minutes. Using a large rubber spatula, gradually fold in the flour, being careful not to deflate the batter.

3. Add about ½ cup of the batter to the melted butter and gently stir until well blended. Fold the butter mixture back into the batter. Pour the batter into the prepared pan, spreading it evenly with the rubber spatula.

4. Bake for 11 to 13 minutes, until the cake is golden brown and the top springs back when lightly pressed. Transfer the pan to a wire rack to cool for 5 minutes. Sprinkle a large clean kitchen towel generously with confectioners' sugar. Run a knife around the edges of the cake to loosen it from the pan, then invert it onto the towel. Carefully peel off the waxed paper, then replace it loosely on the cake. Starting from a long side, roll up the cake, jelly-roll fashion, in the towel. Place seam side down on the rack to cool completely. (The cake can be baked up to 1 day ahead, wrapped in plastic when thoroughly cooled, and stored at room temperature.)

5. Make the chocolate frosting. In a food processor, process the chocolate until finely ground. In a medium saucepan, bring the cream and butter just to a boil, stirring occasionally until the butter is melted. With the motor running, pour the hot cream through the feed tube and process just until the chocolate is melted and the mixture is smooth. Transfer to a medium bowl and stir in the vanilla. Let cool, stirring once or twice, then cover and refrigerate, stirring occasionally, for 1¾ to 2 hours, until thickened and spreadable.

6. Meanwhile, make the whipped cream filling. Combine the chocolate, butter, and 2 tablespoons of the cream in a small saucepan and heat over low heat, stirring frequently, until the chocolate and butter are melted and the mixture is smooth. Transfer to a medium bowl and let cool to room temperature.

7. In a large bowl, combine the remaining 1 cup cream, the sugar, and the vanilla and beat just until soft peaks form; do not overbeat. Stir about ¼ cup of the whipped cream into the cooled chocolate mixture to lighten it, then fold in the remaining cream in 4 or 5 additions.

8. Unroll the cake and remove the waxed paper. Trim about ¼ inch from each side of the cake. Spread the filling evenly over the cake. Starting from a long side, roll up the cake into a compact roll and place seam side down on a large platter (or on a rectangle of heavy cardboard covered with aluminum foil). Cover loosely and refrigerate until ready to frost the cake.

9. To assemble the cake, cut a small diagonal slice off one end and lay the slice, cut side up, slightly off center on the top of the cake, to make a "stump" on the log. Generously frost the cake, including the ends, with the chocolate frosting. If desired, run the tines of a fork down the length of the cake so the frosting resembles tree bark. Cover and refrigerate until shortly before serving time. (The cake can be refrigerated for up to 4 hours.)

10. About 30 minutes before serving (no longer), remove the cake from the refrigerator. To serve, lightly sift confectioners' sugar over the cake, if desired, and slice.

Serves 10 to 12

sherry lemon
molded jelly

MOLDED JELLIES ARE ONE OF THE GREAT English banquet desserts. Royal cooks once spent more time on them than on any other dish of the meal, using elaborate tiered molds for special jewel-tone effects. You'll find this slightly lemony version (so good for digestion) to be the perfect light touch after heavy multi-course holiday meal.

2 cups dry sherry

¼ cup fresh lemon juice (from 2 lemons)

3 packages unflavored gelatin

2 cups sugar

1 ½ cups water

1 ¼ cups white grape juice or apple juice

2 sticks cinnamon, broken into 1-inch pieces

Zest of 1 lemon, removed with a vegetable peeler

6 whole allspice berries

1. In a small metal bowl, stir together ¾ cup of the sherry, the lemon juice, and the gelatin. When the gelatin has softened, place the bowl in a skillet of simmering water until the gelatin dissolves. Remove the skillet from the heat and set it aside, leaving the bowl of gelatin in the hot water.

2. Meanwhile, in a large saucepan, bring the sugar, water, grape juice, cinnamon, zest, and allspice to a boil, stirring until the sugar dissolves; boil for 10 minutes. Remove the pan from the heat and add the gelatin mixture and the remaining 1¼ cups of sherry.

3. Through a fine strainer, pour the mixture into a wet 6-cup ring mold. Let it come to room temperature, cover, and refrigerate until set, at least 6 hours or for up to 3 days.

4. To unmold, dip the mold into hot water for just a few seconds and dry it with paper towels. Place a well-chilled inverted serving plate over the top of the mold and with both hands holding the plate and the mold tightly together, turn them over and remove the mold. Serve immediately.

Serves 8

sesame seed
honey candy

tHE SECRET TO MAKING THESE CLASSIC Chanukkah candies is using fresh, high-quality sesame seeds. Find yours at a health food or specialty store with a good turnover. Wrap up these crunchy treats in colored cellophane in traditional colors of the holiday—blue, white, and silver—pack in a like-colored tin, and present to guests as gifts.

¾ **cup honey**

¼ **teaspoon ground cinnamon**

Pinch of salt

1 ½ **cups (about 8 ounces) hulled (white)**
   sesame seeds

1 **cup blanched almonds, finely chopped**

1. Line a 13- x 9-inch baking pan with foil, allowing it to extend over the short ends of the pan, and generously oil the foil. Set the pan on a heatproof surface.

2. In a large heavy skillet, bring the honey to a rolling boil over medium heat. Add the cinnamon and salt, stir in the sesame seeds, and cook, stirring constantly with a wooden spoon, until the seeds begin to color, about 3 minutes. Add the almonds and stir until evenly coated, then immediately scrape the mixture into the prepared pan. Using the back of the spoon, spread it as evenly as possible in the pan. (Once the candy has cooled slightly, you can flatten it again with your fingertips if you like.) Let the candy cool until it is lukewarm.

3. Using the foil, lift the slab of candy out of the pan, invert it onto a cutting board, and peel off the foil. Turn the candy over and, using a sharp heavy knife, cut into 1-inch squares. Let cool completely. Store the candies between layers of waxed paper in an airtight container at room temperature. (The candy will keep for several days.)

Makes 8 dozen candies

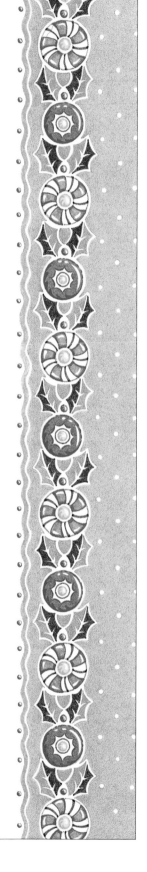

holiday mulled
cider

WHAT BRINGS MERRIMENT ON (AND WARDS off Jack Frost) more quickly than mulled cider? Mix up a batch and let the cozy fragrance spread warmth through your rooms faster than a fleece blanket. Make the kids their own brew without the brandy.

2 quarts apple cider or juice

1 lemon, thinly sliced

2 tablespoons light brown sugar

2 cinnamon sticks

12 whole allspice berries

12 whole cloves

6 lady apples or thick apple slices

1 cup applejack or apple brandy (optional)

1. In a Dutch oven, bring the cider, lemon, sugar, cinnamon sticks, and allspice to a boil over medium-high heat. Reduce the heat to low and simmer for 10 minutes.

2. Insert 2 cloves into each of the apples. Add the apples and applejack to the cider and heat for 2 minutes.

Serves 8

Butter Baking Basics

For baking, most bakers prefer unsalted butter because it allows them to control the amount of salt in the recipe. Unsalted butter does not last as long as salted, so be sure to check the date when buying and before using. Also, read the label to be sure it contains eighty percent fat. Any less means there's a higher percentage of water, which is not recommended for baking. If you substitute shortening for butter, use only unflavored solid vegetable shortening.

To soften butter, remove it from the refrigerator and place an unwrapped stick between two sheets of wax paper. With a rolling pin, give each side of the butter a few whacks to make it pliable; let stand at room temperature until it is the consistency of raw cookie dough.

cranberry-orange
sparkling punch

tOAST THE NEW YEAR (OR ANY HOLIDAY) with this fizzy, bubbly punch. With all those pretty mint sprigs and orange slices bobbing about, you'll want to show it off in a cut-crystal punch bowl.

> 1 quart (4 cups) cranberry juice cocktail, chilled
>
> ½ cup orange juice
>
> 1 bottle Champagne or other dry sparkling
>   wine, chilled
>
> Ice cubes
>
> Mint sprigs, orange slices, and cranberries, for garnish

In a large bowl, combine the cranberry juice and orange juice. Slowly add the Champagne. Transfer to a punch bowl, add ice cubes, and garnish with the mint and orange slices.

Serves 8

◆ Nonalcoholic Punch

Substitute 3 cups chilled ginger ale for the Champagne.

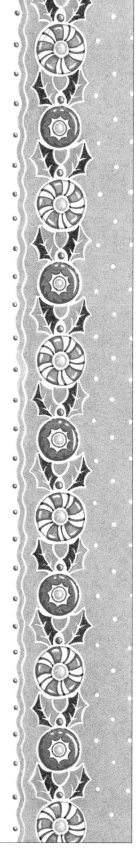

index

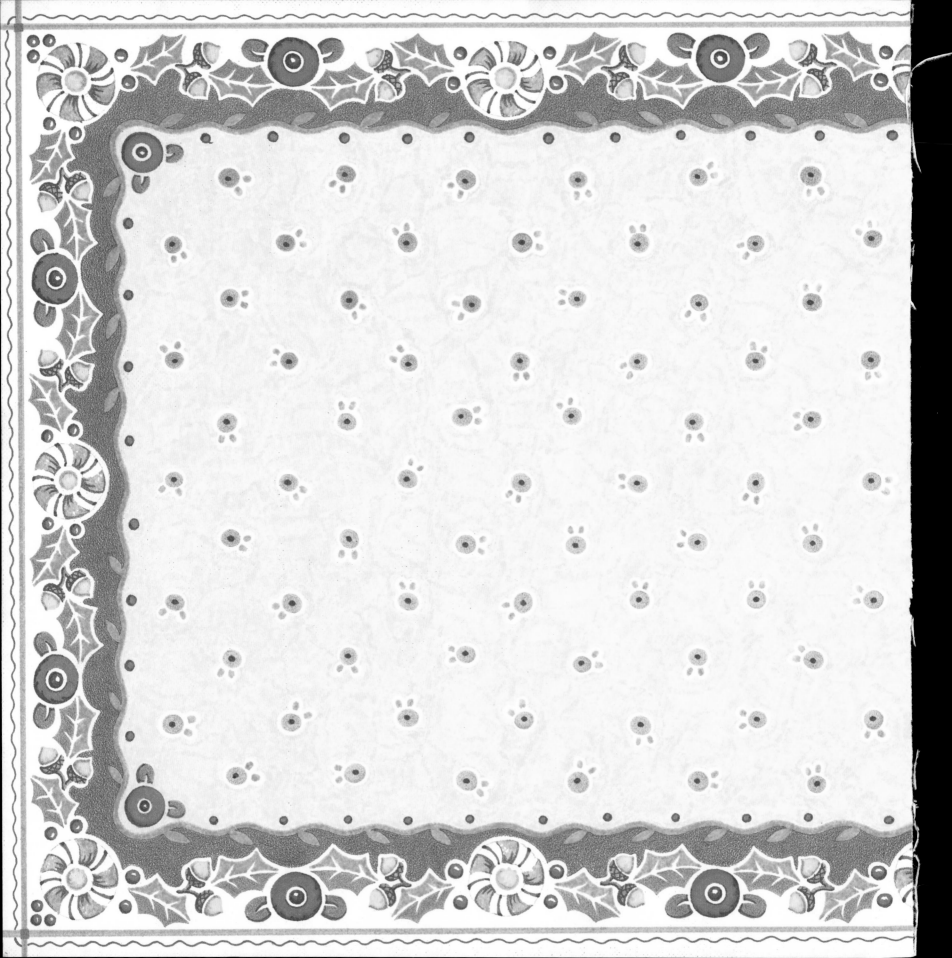